The Wonderful World of VenhoevenCS Architects

THE WONDERFUL WORLD OF

VenhoevenCS

Architects

episode publishers, Rotterdam 2009

This publication has been made possible with the generous support of the Netherlands Architecture Fund, Rotterdam

Compilation: Ton Venhoeven, Pieter Jan Gijsberts, Jos-Willem van Oorschot, Helga Lasschuijt, Lydia Fraaije, Tim Habraken, Bas Römgens, Janneke van der Poel

Text contributions: Ton Venhoeven, Pieter Jan Gijsberts, Bernard Colenbrander, Wim Nijenhuis, Pnina Avidar, Marc Schoonderbeek, Tim Habraken, Helga Lasschuijt, Bas Römgens, Ineke van der Burg

Text editing and proofreading: VenhoevenCS, Eleonoor Jap Sam, Christopher Nicolson
Image editing: VenhoevenCS, Simon Davies
Translation and proofreading: Gerard van den Hooff, George Hall, Ron de Klerk
Design: Simon Davies with the assistance of Fanny Batmale, Stefan Hanser and Allen Smithee
Printing and lithography: Thieme MediaCenter, Rotterdam
Photo credits: All photos and images by VenhoevenCS except: Luuk Kramer: p. 64, 70, 94-95, 96, 97, 100, 101, 105, 150-151, 152, 155, 159, 160, 162, 163, 164-165, 215, 216, 217, 238-239, 240, 241, 242, 243, 245, 259, 260, 263, 264, 267, 268-269, 270, 271. Rob Marinissen: pp. 66-67. Flickr, Jaap Keller: p. 67. Jorgen Koopmanschap: pp. 68-69. Flickr, Roevin: p. 71. P. Eelenbaas: p. 72. Flickr, Else Kramer: p. 72. Flickr, Roy del Vecchio: p. 72. Sjur Aartun: p. 73. Flickr, Arne Kuilman: p. 74. Flickr, vanderveenr: p. 74. Flickr, Carst van der Molen: p. 77. Simon Davies: p. 81. Rob Hoekstra: p. 152, 219, 220, 221, 254-255, 263, 265, 266. OKRA: p. 159. Copijn: p. 160, 161. Marjoleine Boonstra: p. 181, 182, 184, 185, 186, 187, 188, 190-191, 192-193, 199, 207, 209, 210, 212-213. Joost Brouwers: p. 204, 209. Martin Thomas: 205. René de Wit: p. 251, 252.

For inspiration and explanation of projects, VenhoevenCS works with references and sources from all over the world. We gratefully use the Internet, newspaper archives and books on various subjects in our design process. As explained on pages 168 and 169 in notes 37, 38 and 39, we consider appropriating and transforming these pictures by using them in a new network of meaning, as essential event in cultural evolution. The concept of this book was to make this working method visible to the reader. To make clear that we used those pictures as mere samples, most referential pictures were compressed and converted to black and white images. Credits of all other reference pictures are listed above. Selection of inspirational works: Cotta Vaz, Marc & Hata, Shinji, The Star Wars Archives: Props, Costumes, Models and Artwork from Star Wars (lucasfilm); Dunster, David, Architectural Monographs 4: Alvar Aalto (London: Academy Editions, 1978); Gudis, Catherine, Helter Skelter: LA art in the 1990s (Los Angeles: Museum of Contemporary Art, 1992); Günay, Rehe, Sinan The architect and his works (Yem Yahin, 1998); Nijenhuis, W. and Nio, M. EATING BRAZIL (Rotterdam: 010 Publishers, 1999); Tod, Ian & Wheeler, Michael, Utopia (Bussum: Unieboek, 1979); Vollemans, Kees, Dieren Demonen (Zwolle: Waanders, 1993)

episode publishers, Rotterdam
www.episode-publishers.nl

www.venhoevencs.nl

ISBN 978-90-5973-073-1

5
Contents

Introduction

Long live the Internet: everywhere one can feel the seduction to scroll through the daily offers of an unlimited number of websites offering inspiration and knowledge from long gone times and formerly far away cultures. Also the tourism and entertainment industry offer plenty opportunities for a quick trip to a different world. Globalization and high tech virtualization enter the everyday and alter our definition of context. Today, the world is our village and playground. For architects, artists and composers, the impulse to make outstanding work for a specific location and time, a concept that inspired so many in the good old days, seems to have lost its sex appeal. Globalization changes our local culture and the environment that we live in.

The Wonderful World of VenhoevenCS Architects is not only the first monograph on the works of VenhoevenCS architects, but also a thematic essay dealing with this new reality: the problems it causes and the opportunities it offers.

The essay engages the problems, because for the world, it is not all fun. It addresses problems like climate change, soil exhaustion, population growth, massive migration and many ethnic and cultural conflicts fuelled by the worldwide demand for natural resources. By the end of this century, ten to fifteen billion humans will want to consume ten times more than today, whereas today, we already consume more than the earth can provide. In architecture and city planning, holding on to outdated or newly invented cultural identities, as many seem to propose, does not bring a solution to the aforementioned problems any closer. We cannot return to a world population of five hundred million; the time of isolated territories with their own separated cultures is long gone. Instead, innovations are required from technicians and more dynamic and complex cultural concepts must be developed by architects. We need to reconsider our habits in city planning and architecture.

The essay also engages the opportunities, because globalization and the Internet provide both the cultural exchange and the extended scientific networks we need to get the information and innovation required to develop 'ecosolutions' for tomorrow. With this book we want to contribute to the open source development of those solutions.

That is why we share background information, ideas, technical developments and many cultural concepts with our readers.

The Wonderful World of VenhoevenCS Architects shows our designs and explanatory texts in the context of a number of critical essays, references and suggestions for further reading. Presenting our designs, we felt it was no longer suitable to include only information and pictures of the buildings and their physical environment as a referential framework for the reader, so we reproduced their globalized cultural context instead. Hundreds of pictures from all over the world, the essays and the bits and pieces of text are used to recreate this complex environment.

By means of a number of classifications we have split up our oeuvre into subsets. These classifications: network machines, micro networks and events, bodies, skins, herds and images and microcosms, reflect the telescopic view, the various scale levels of the projects and the central themes in our work. Each time the different projects have been lumped together under a common denominator and each project works out that denominator in a different manner. This is how the different forms of that denominator are given their due. In this way the classifications mix and complement each other. In addition, icons are used to refer to themes that are found in the designs and sometimes a separate text is devoted to them. Numbers and icons in texts and pictures allow for a smooth navigation through the book as if it were a web browser. It can be read superficially by looking at the pictures and scanning some highlighted words and titles. One can read fragments or just one essay, or one can really study it and continue reading all suggested literature. The storyline is roughly the same. The Wonderful World of VenhoevenCS Architects can be seen as a network, an urban structure where all things somehow refer to each other.

With this book we seek to build bridges between different worlds. We want to make the politician understand the carpenter and the economist understand the artist. Some people have a talent for visual information, others rely mostly on words. It is impossible to imagine our culture today without images and for many people images are a more accessible way of understanding stories; this is why we make liberal use of visual material to transfer information. For people with a visual intelligence this monograph is a graphic novel. For others the word is a better medium. Hence we have incorporated extensive texts to provide the study with comments. The word does not function solely to support the image, nor does the image serve as a mere illustration of the text. Both tell stories that touch on the work without fully representing it. The work is what it is and for this reason drawings and photographs of the various projects have been incorporated to offer the reader the opportunity to interpret the work in his own way.

Architecture is not the illustration of ill-comprehended philosophy, but a practice of making places where concepts from different worlds and cultures meet. Innovation in a project is the result of dialogue and co-operation between people participating in the design process. Architecture is about use and transformation by appropriation of elements from the cultural context of past and present. This book shows what is done in practice by clients and advisers in terms of theory development, what practicable aspects are hidden in different popular and mass cultures and what is possible if views from different realities are combined. In the various projects not only our own ideas, but also those of clients, politicians, local residents and urban developers have been incorporated. In the continuous interview text, such backgrounds of the realization of the various projects are elucidated.

The Wonderful World of VenhoevenCS Architects is not only a presentation of designs and a reconstruction of contexts; it aims to reflect on the everyday reality of globalization as well. This publication is a monograph with a prominent role for theory. The various texts, designs and references to different domains of reality are also used to show, stimulate and provoke possible new directions in the development of our very diverse cultures. Also, we have asked four authors, Bernard Colenbrander, Wim Nijenhuis, Pnina Avidar and Marc Schoonderbeek to shed more light on the theoretical context of our work. They show where our ideas touch on existing theory.

Bernard Colenbrander sets about by elucidating how representation works in architecture, how in the past people thought of references to nature and the cosmos. He then goes on to explain how those 'references' fell into abeyance and were increasingly replaced by instrumental (utilitarian) architecture. By that time, architecture could no longer confine itself to demonstrating interrelationships with nature and cosmos, but had to play a part in society; architecture had to make a goal attainable. Architecture is then beginning to perform as a machine, an instrument that enables man to come to grips with his environment, with which he can control the world. Colenbrander makes the next step on the basis of Peter Sloterdijk's body of ideas. He explains how the notion and wish to control the world by means of buildings and objects have reached a deadlock, ending in a baroque entirety of machines that never do exactly what you had in mind. Colenbrander situates our work in this world – which from 'a broad attempt to control' has changed into 'an uncontrollable, catastrophic heteromobility: a bewildering avalanche crashing down towards the valley with a thundering roar'. He concludes by stating that 'VenhoevenCS does not make machines to control the world, but objects that represent the cosmos in all its uncontrollability.'

Wim Nijenhuis feels that the objects, the cities, the people, have degenerated into pure, unambiguous articles. On account of this condition they can circulate ever easier and faster: there is no need to dwell on something at great length, for 'what you see is what you get'. The space in which these articles circulate is a 'smooth' space that is above all quantifiable. Gone is the space of representation, the space that is illusory, the space between sign and object, the interspace. Nijenhuis argues passionately that this interspace of representation must be reclaimed. The role of the spectator in this is essential. In the smooth space, the user is a hyp-

10

notized being, a dead robot. In the space of representation the spectator has to set to work on the interspace, combining his own experiences with the signs and objects. In this way the flexible connection between what something is and what it seems, can be severed and this in its turn may give rise to hitches. Here, in this hiatus, space can be created for everyday events and the development of life.

The author-couple Pnina Avidar and Marc Schoonderbeek wrote a text in three parts that touches on the idea that language and representation are ambiguous instruments that create a reality of their own. The first part explains how architecture forms a framework for daily life. Within this framework the heavenly, the everyday and the underworld are combined. Architecture is a definition of place with the help of existing images. In the second part the point of view shifts to life and movement. Here attention is drawn to the role played by the various languages in the realization of a work of architecture. In addition Avidar and Schoonderbeek set out how modernism tried to fixate the identity of people and objects to turn them into components for machines with controlling functions. With the crisis of modernism this attempt is smashed into an endless series of differences. In the third and last part, Deleuze's f o l d is brought to the fore. For Deleuze the f o l d is the representation of constant movement in the development of life. Here their essay turns into a cultural argument to take the plunge into the unknown.

Today, the different cultures of the world are home to different realities that, because of our shrinking world, become more and more mixed-up. Many languages are spoken at the same time, even in one and the same discussion. These are not only the languages of various migrated and migrating people. The different languages of everyday life for example, are not only shaped by different everyday experiences, but also by a myriad of spectacles, films, mythologies and amusement parks. Also, every culture has the different languages of economists, physicists and philosophers. The resulting many different cultures of the world have their own ideals and understandings, interpretations, illusions and misapprehensions and they all influence the unpredictable development of the culture of globalization.

In spite of all these seemingly autonomous languages, architecture is still closely tied up with many social and cultural issues at the same time. In our work, for example, modes of thought from a wide range of disciplines, such as biology, physics, economics, mechanical engineering, history, archaeology and futurology are connected with mythology, art, philosophy, theories of aesthetics and politics to shape the environment for everyday life. Sometimes in a straightforward manner, sometimes surreptitiously, along stealthy roundabout ways and by vague allusions. With each project we attempt to build bridges between different practices and theories. Not by illustrating theory with a specific design, but by somehow or other creating interrelationships between practices with varying backgrounds. By appropriating individual languages and theories for various subjects, our practice is coming about.

In the course of designing, we have developed many concepts and discovered, used and transformed a variety of exceptional ideas from other disciplines that we would like to communicate in a different way – a way that is clearer and more comprehensible to a broader public. The fact is that architecture is an awkward and slow medium to make the contribution of practice to the development of ideas of culture more explicit. With The Wonderful World of VenhoevenCS Architects we are better able to show in what way we participate in the culture of globalization and what position we hold within all controversial discussions surrounding the issue.

Around us we observe an increasingly constrained demeanour as a consequence of unsuccessful attempts to come to grips with the world of globalization. No stone is left unturned to make the world around us controllable, while it is becoming more and more evident that this is bound to fail. Too many people from too many different backgrounds try to control it with too many instruments. Meanwhile we are saddled with all kinds of objects and things intended to perform all kinds of actions, but which stopped to serve any clear purpose a long time ago. This publication shows how architecture in this context can be more than just an instrument to control the world, its events, spaces, people, animals and its things.

As a reaction to the increasing awareness of the uncontrollability of our space, we would like to point out that a notion such as 'chance' is beginning to show philosophical features. Chance can easily get bogged down in the view that this is the way of the world and that there is nothing anyone can do about it, as if we are left to the tender mercy of fate. We want to demonstrate that there is a way out of the constrained attempt to make the world controllable as well as of the paralysing relegation to fate. Our view is simple: cause new events, develop a taste for new perspectives, enjoy the moment, embrace encounters, accept uncontrollability and explore the unknown. In doing so, we will all be expected to adopt a new role, viz. in becoming active participants in the design and use of the world, so that our environment is not only defined by the laws and patterns of language and the economy, but also by our passions, experiences, and actions.

This is an interactive book. Though it contains many explanations and references aiming at clarifying the cultural and physical context of our designs and the complexity of architectural practice in general, it also offers too many of them, creating information gaps and overlaps: plenty opportunities for the reader to complement the texts and images with his own illusionary content, private life experiences and chance associations. As a result, the book is not only a representation of our work but also a new cultural subject, waiting to be appropriated and concurred by the reader. As if it were a living object.

Ton Venhoeven

Works of nature and of the mind
Bernard Colenbrander

In contrast with the past, anyone with a message to convey in today's culture would sooner choose images rather than words. The academic argument, with all its logic and chronology, has given way to a succession of colourful images, depicted in every impressionistic kind of variety. PowerPoint technology is now accessible to all and can turn the most tedious scientific issue or the dullest bureaucratic procedure into a painless adventure. Whatever the communicative advantages of images may be, by reversing what used to be the essentials and what the illustration, we have not made establishing an argument's special gravity any easier. Visual culture, on the other hand, offers a much richer source of moods and subjective messages than any argument based on classic logic could ever contain. And so, the public – looking for experience rather than knowledge – is approached in suitable fashion.

In the field of architecture (a science traditionally at the crossroads of subjective representation and objective theory and technology) this visual prominence has also left its marks. A lecture on architecture nowadays consists of a staccato of scenes from within and without the field and goes far beyond the conventional presentations accompanied by slides of buildings and designs. As such, they compare to many contemporary architecture magazines and monographies; these, too, lean towards indefinable comprehensive formats of complete variation, a variation not – at least not merely – tedious or destructive, but reflective of the current practice of architecture. The field is exposed to considerable social pressure at a time when new formats for the division of labour increasingly impede the consistency and personal signature of architectural designs. Occasionally, the pressure is such that it rouses the desire to break through the traditional walls of architecture (in the sense of the historically rooted culture of building) and create a wider social and scientific foundation that allows for greater operational freedom, if need be at the expense of the traditional unambiguity of the design process.

'Offices that are ambitious and comprehensive', Ole Bouman wrote in A r c h i s, 'are often also powerhouses of new talents, laboratories for experiments and as such, act similarly as schools. They may also start publicity campaigns that organize 'relevance' in its own right.'[1] And why should architecture remain architecture as such? This, at least, appears to be the assumption of these explorative movements. Would it not be better, so their assumption continues, for architecture to evolve into something different, now that the actual building process turns out to be the most frustrating part of the trade?

It remains to be seen what the chances of success are for this kind of expansionism, a development meant to bring the field into an operational alliance with centres of politics and science. For the time being, it is interesting to note that the way in which architecture is practised these days has acutely motivated some to embrace a renewed theoretical involvement with the world a r o u n d the building process, specifically with the sociology and philosophy of the current human condition.

It is precisely this new involvement, which marks the starting point of this essay. The case of the young architecture firm VenhoevenCS, formed by Ton Venhoeven, is more than incidental. It illustrates a new complex of inspiring images and theories, leading to a number of unusual approaches to what exactly constitutes a building; approaches that even extend to include production techniques. At the same time, the design and construction remain the essence of the work. There are, as is usual, the various references indicating the genetic blueprint of the work. In the case of Venhoeven, these references come in the form of a series of wide-ranging inspirations, as becomes clear from the colourful PowerPoint presentation he uses to explain his work. At the start, we are shown an orange, float-

1. See: A r c h i s (2005, no. 1), 'Volume no. 1: 'Architecture m u s t go beyond itself', Ole Bouman, 'Architecture as harmless practice or ...', p. 10

ing freely in the air, depicted as a perfect sphere with a gently spotlighted texture. Another sphere follows, but this one is completely artificial and apparently created as a suggestive environment for a science fiction movie. After reviewing the three-dimensional, and rather outlandish, reality we can now see some aerial shots of a cave that was made accessible and inhabitable by carving out shapes with holes in them. Then follows a colourful textile patchwork, photographed lying flat, and, again representing the science fiction department, several spaceships in flight. Next is the cut-away model of an Apple computer and the aerodynamically integrated headlights of a sports car. Finally, we see the torso of a woman in a finely pleated garment on which is printed the figure of another woman, apparently taken from a historic painting: one body covering the other. The images evoke a universe where artificial and organic components combine into erratic scenes. Content and form interact continuously, although the skin of the objects that populate this universe is ambiguous about both.

The transition from images to buildings – for this firm, too, they form the heart of their production – happens flawlessly, almost unnoticeably. Several designs are represented as a series of custom-built components, around which the 'casing' is fitted, equally built-to-size. Once you interpret the image as that of some machine, the continuing association is hard to avoid. From a certain perspective, these could be taken for animals; the outer skin is smooth in one design, rough in another. Forms are pulled around, gently, without clearly defined horizontal or vertical lines.

While a traditional building is based on the Cartesian axis system, Venhoeven's designs are laid out in more unrestricted patterns, stacked and folded. We can see a bridge inclining towards the other side in a crawling movement, making it an event as much as a construction. We are also shown buildings literally sheeted in a verdant landscape. Here and there, the landscape penetrates the building, forming an entire artificial jungle. They are indeed buildings, but they don't seem to conform to any convention relating to buildings.

In approaching the natural world and the mechanical world, buildings like these distance themselves remarkably from the architectural tradition. More so than conventional buildings, these are constructed landscapes of a rather alienating quality. It inspires curiosity as to the thematic origin of this concept. Do these buildings reach back in time, circumventing the long-established architectural standard, intent on reclaiming the most primitive naturalistic foundation of the architectural tradition? Was the architect in search of some vital source, putting aside the entire accumulated knowledge of centuries? One might easily entertain such an idea, because these buildings do not resemble what is usually considered a building. Or could the focus for this architectural work lie in the opposite direction, towards an unknown and ominous future?

This raises the question of what the motive could be for manoeuvring away from the established tradition. To come closer to answering this question, one cannot simply skip exploring the genealogy of the traditional concept of architecture. Perhaps it is in the sequence of moments in the history of architectural evolution that we can find motive to help appreciate the camouflage in the VenhoevenCS' building designs. It may be especially useful to draw parallels between those moments in time where architecture acts both as a representative medium (that is, when a building can be explained as an interpretation of a non-architectural reality) and the naturalistic and alienating trend of recent times, a trend with which the Venhoeven's designs move in sync.

The classical architectural canon was created in the course of an irregular process that took centuries and developed into an impressive genealogy of architectural grammar. Inherent to this grammar was an organic foundation that reflected the natural landscape. Architectural theory has emphasized from the start that the Doric order (which constituted the heart of the vocabulary that the ancient Greeks created) was originally based on primitive predecessors in wood, and that a temple's architecture simply reflected the dimensions of the human body. This then, was the starting point of a gruesomely protracted process of stylizing, modifying, and expanding: a mere idea, literally rooted in the nature of things – the landscape and the human figure – was developed into an autonomous architectural order.

The generic principles were provided – at least in the western world – by the ancient Greeks, both for the architecture of individual buildings as for the layout of a city. How these principles were actualized over time may be reconstructed sequentially from what antiquity has left us. Archaeology has provided us with the hardest data, but this science generally doesn't give us much insight into the phenomenological significance of the Greek and subsequent Roman vocabulary: the way it appeared and was experienced as soon as it was expressed via buildings, statues, streets, squares, and city walls.

In the nineteen twenties, the paucity of historical information in this genre led Marguerite Yourcenar to embark on a reconstruction of a most intriguing chapter of antiquity: the life of the Roman Emperor Hadrian. It was to take her half a century to produce a result to her satisfaction: from extinct documents she distilled the memories, opinions, and moods of the Emperor, and, where necessary, fills these in with her own interpretations. In this recreated memoir, Hadrian's thoughts frequently wander off to the city's culture: 'Each time that I have looked from afar, at the bend of some sunny road, toward a Greek acropolis with its perfect city fixed to the hill like a flower to its stem,' Yourcenar has the emperor say, 'I could not but feel that the incomparable plant was limited by its very perfection, achieved on one point of space and in one segment of time. Its sole chance of expansion, as for that of a plant, was in its seed; with the pollen of its ideas Greece has fertilized the world.'[2]

After having considered the Greeks Hadrian now drew his own conclusions. 'But Rome, less light and less shapely, sprawling to the plain at her river's edge, was moving toward vaster growth: the city has become the State. I should have wished the State to expand still more, likening itself to the order of the universe, to the divine nature of things. Virtues which had sufficed for the small city of the Seven Hills would have to grow less rigid and more varied if they were to meet the needs of all the earth. ... When I was visiting ancient cities, sacred but wholly dead, and without present value for the human race, I promised myself to save this Rome of mine from the petrification of a Thebes, a Babylon, or a Tyre. She would no longer be bound by her body of stone, but would compose for herself from the words State, citizenry, and republic a surer immortality. In the countries as yet untouched by our culture, on the banks of the

2. Marguerite Yourcenar, Memoirs of Hadrian, tr. Grace Frick (Gordonsville, VA: Farrar, Straus and Giroux, 1990 (1963)), pp. 109-111

Rhine and the Danube, or the shores of the Batavian Sea, each village enclosed within its wooden palisade brought to mind the reed hut and dunghill where our Roman twins had slept content, fed by the milk of the wolf; these cities-to-be would follow the pattern of Rome.'

In Yourcenar's vivid explanation of the Roman emperor's motivation and way of seeing, the budding Greek concept fanned out over an entire continent and was applied to serve immense geopolitical aspirations: building turned city turned state. Architecture became representation; in abstracto, it embodied a structure of far greater dimensions that itself. For the architectural grammar specifically, the application was focussed on the significance of the building orders: these were to be adapted in both a spatial and a typological sense for use in the larger and differentiated urban arrangements of the Romans. In the process, the orders were transformed into 'pure ornamentation', in the words of art historian Rudolf Wittkower.[3] The Romans applied the orders into compositions of arch and vault constructions hitherto unknown to the Greeks, thus clearing the road for multi-storey buildings. The typological range was also expanded from the temple to a rich choice in buildings, all of which were assigned their place in the rational layout of the Roman city. This Roman city, always identical in composition all over the continent, was among the principal vehicles of the Roman Empire's geopolitical aspirations.

In the evolution of classical architecture from Greek to Roman, and later from the Roman era to the Renaissance, the shifting view on the function of columns and walls is one of the most visible links. Some views remained unchanged, like that of identifying the concepts of city and state. But where the Romans had already put the prominence of the column into perspective, it was Alberti who, in the early Renaissance, took the next step. Alberti considered, 'a row of columns nothing more ... than a discontinuous wall that is open in some places.' Because he saw an arcade as an [open wall], he was able to transform, in the course of his life, the classical architecture elements and allow them to function in what Wittkower called 'a consistent wall architecture'.[4]

3. Rudolf Wittkower, Architectural Priciples in the Age of Humanism, (London: Academy Editions, 1973), pp. 33-56
4. Ibid., p. 47

This transformation of the antique grammar into a wall architecture ena-bled the field to apply a much more liberal, subjective design, in which the constructional aspects of the traditional orders largely disappeared. By abandoning the way the old masters had applied the orders, architec-ture had broken free from its own naturalistic origins. In coming of age it developed an ever differentiated and independent classical grammar – a source of experiment throughout the western world since Alberti, which, is, even today, considered the most monumental of all architecture's con-tributions to cultural history.

It may sound out of place to discuss the evolution of ancient architecture, from 'column architecture' to 'wall architecture', in an essay dealing with an oeuvre that is so quintessentially contemporary. It may be even less obvious to do so now that this oeuvre so clearly seems to want to move outside the established genealogical path.

And above all, the classical impulse has long ended, ever since it became clear, in the course of the nineteenth century that it was incompatible with the many-headed mechanized monster called modernity. No matter how obsolete the classical ideas may be, many agree that they can still be seen as inspiring, including Ignasi de Solà-Morales, a theorist closely in-volved in emerging architecture movements until his early death in 2001.[5] Maybe not everybody will be inspired by the concrete grammar of build-ings dating from antiquity or the Renaissance, but more so by the power-ful evolutionary demonstration of classical architecture. Architecture can carry far-reaching meanings across very long periods of time, meanings going back to experiences that were once deeply rooted in nature.

In comparison, the history of modern architecture after 1800 is a tale of loss and erosion. With modernity on the march, the classical notion that architecture should reflect the structure of the cosmos was pushed into the background. The belief that building, city, and state form one ideal unit, seen as relevant until long after Alberti, narrowed and died. As an ex-ception, the utopian voice of Aldo van Eyck echoed far into the twentieth

5. Ignasi de Solà-Morales, Differences: Topographies of contemporary architecture (Cambridge: MIT Press, 1999 (1997)), p. 58. The classical tradition is referred to here as 'something that still inspires'.

century, speaking in grand naturalistic analogies of tree, house, and city.[6] Likewise there was, earlier in the same century, Frank Lloyd Wright, who believed 'that the secret of all the human styles in architecture was the same that gave character to trees'.[7]

Van Eyck and Wright were prominent among generations that derived their direct inspiration from the characteristic spirit of contemporary culture rather than the chronic whispers of the primeval forest. This contemporary culture in turn held motifs for representation and even for straightforward illusionism in architecture, although these motifs did not find their direct origin in a representation of a primeval natural world. For the time being, the 'primitive hut' remained in the distance, at least as a direct source of inspiration or contemporary architecture. Much more pronounced was the focus on the contemporary social programme, particularly with daily life in the modern Western world changing so drastically.

Embracing mass housing projects in the newly formed metropoles, architecture became an applied art form more than ever before. This applied art brought the world of architecture closer to that of the purely functional, as could be seen in the work J.J.P. Oud, the most ideologically distinctive modernist in the Netherlands of the early twentieth-century. Oud spoke of automobiles, ocean liners, yachts, menswear, sportswear, electrical appliances, toiletries, and utensils as a direct source of inspiration for the tasks his generation faced, for these objects, so he said, 'being the purest reflection of their time, harbour the rudimentary elements of a new aesthetic design and may be considered the starting point for the outward appearance of the new art.'[8]

In this view, architecture should reflect the design of functional objects and, in doing so, become less building and more appliance. Another characteristic theme of modernism emerged: apart from the new involvement

6. See Francis Strauven, Aldo van Eyck: relativiteit en verbeelding (Amsterdam: Meulenhoff, 1994), p. 404

7. Quoted from: Michael Kimmelman, 'The dreams of Frank Lloyd Wright', in: The New York Review of Books (2005, no. 13), p. 45

8. J.J.P. Oud, 'Over de toekomstige bouwkunst en hare architectonische mogelijkheden', in: Bouwkundig Weekblad (1921), pp. 147-160

with the social programme of its time, compositions in modernist architecture were also elicited by changes in spatial ideals. The old-fashioned building, in its physical manifestation, rested heavily on the ground. From the mid-nineteenth century onwards, the availability of new construction techniques and materials enabled the gradual introduction of its counterpart: the optically suspended building. Suddenly, Vitruvian qualities like usefulness and stability were less relevant than before. When spans, for example, were stretched to such a degree that capsizing seemed inevitable, this considerably upset the visual relationship between structure and form. Space itself rather than the elements controlling a space became a theme in this kind of architecture.

Oud referred to a 'visual characteristic that is optically immaterial, almost suspended'.[9] And that was merely the beginning. In the experiments of Van Doesberg and Van Eesteren, for instance, or those of Le Corbusier, the static quality and set point of view made way for a four-dimensional composition, staged for an observer in constant motion and who was now suddenly envisioned as a pedestrian. In an imagined building like Van Doesburg and Van Eesteren's renowned Maison Particulière (1923), what once was a composition developed into a proposed routing.

The origin of this four-dimensional aspect of architecture has sometimes been linked to spatial illusion created in eighteen-century Rococo salons, where mirrors were used to suggest a dazzling spatial sequence beyond the actual contours of the room.[10] Whether or not historically inspired, the dynamic, at times erratic expression of early twentieth-century architecture was a characteristic representation of a social order engaged, more than ever before, in programming complex issues in time. Here too, as was the case with the Romans and with Alberti, architecture was the symbolic expression of a constellation larger than a mere building: architecture represented a worldview.

The unravelling of the urban planning issue, as it presents itself in the modern era, has posed one of the most important tasks for those dis-

9. Ibid., p. 159

10. Peter Collins, Changing Ideals in Modern Architecture 1750-1950 (London: Faber and Faber, 1965), p. 27

ciplines that deal with how we organize our society: the history of urban development and urban planning, of course, but also for disciplines that reach far beyond the material theory of forms, like sociology and philosophy. In order to explain the way historic avant-garde architecture and, subsequently, contemporary architecture manifested itself, these latter two disciplines are hard to ignore. For the purpose of identifying the erratic characteristics of architecture, the sweeping philosophical work of Peter Sloterdijk (focusing ever more on the spatial expression of the prevailing philosophical system with each new volume) seems to be the most appropriate. Even before he started his by now well-known trilogy S p h e r e s, he presented (in his book E u r o t a o i s m u s from 1989) a compact analyses of philosophical characteristics of the modern era, an analysis that may easily be applied to the field of architecture. In this work, Sloterdijk compares the mentality in pre-modern times with that of the modern era. In pre-modern times, humans had yet to take fate into their own hands, and were merely directed by the erratic compass of the supreme being, whose whims and cruelties cannot be fathomed but merely accepted in all their capriciousness. A fundamental passivity marked the human perspective. 'Kommt es normal, dann kommt es anders – das ist das Apriori der altweltlichten praktische Lebenserfahrung'. But the dawning of Modernism changed all that and the perspective was shifting. 'Mit dem Anbruch der Moderne aber kommt es neu, so, wie Menschen es gedacht haben. Es kommt wie gedacht, weil westliche Menschen, Mönche, Kaufleute, Ärzte, Architekten, Maler und Kanonengießer – in s u m m a Genies und Ingenieure – sich daran machen, ihr Denken neu zu organisieren.' [11] In the modern era, the technical and administrative complex of the planning process replaced the earlier ecology of power and impotence. The future was now rendered predictable; 'being able to' was now balanced with 'wanting to', mostly by mastering the working of social mechanisms.

Modernity is entirely focussed on controlling events in time, no matter how complex a system this requires. 'Der Projektcharakter dieses Neuen Zeitalters resultiert aus der großartigen Unterstellung, man könne in ihm den Weltlauf bald so laufen machen, daß sich nur noch das bewegt was wir durch unsere eigenen Aktivitäten vernünftigerweise in Gang halten

11. Peter Sloterdijk, E u r o t a o i s m u s : Z u r K r i t i k d e r p o l i t i s c h e n K i n e t i k (Frankfurt am Main: Suhrkamp, 1989), p. 21

wollen. Das Projekt der Moderne gründet somit – das ist noch nie scharf ausgesprochen worden – in einer <u>k i n e t i s c h e n   U t o p i e</u>.' [12]

This idea of a kinetic utopia is pivotal in the diagnosis Sloterdijk commits to his battle to understand modernity's ambitions. 'Kinetic' in this respect primarily means created or organized in time: history is made controllable in its progression while the course of nature is adjusted in the process, with the technical sciences playing a lead role. Typical of Sloterdijk's own post-modern position is that he lets the clouds gather as soon as he has formulated his diagnosis of controllability. This modern ambition to control and plan every aspect of society creates immediate conflicts with every negation of disruption of the system it encounters, as it gradually does, for instance, when new techniques are introduced. 'Was sich da zu einer ungewohnten Problemwelt auffaltet, sind die Paradoxien des neuweltlichen Prozesses selbst: Über die Geschichte schiebt sich ein Posthistoire, über die Natur eine Epinatur, über die Moderne eine Postmoderne.' [13]

It is the movement in the determined system itself that can create local uncontrollability in the course of the process. 'Es sind Dinge ins Rollen gekommen (auch andere als Roltreppen), die man keinesfalls vorhergesehen hat', Sloterdijk argues, which can easily turn a grand attempt to control events into an uncontrollable, catastrophic heteromobility: a bewildering avalanche thundering down the hill.

This change, of a meticulously programmed project becoming a not or hardly controllable sequence of facts and event, is not some philosophical abstraction; it has manifested itself broadly in our recent past. Relatively innocent may be the way our (once so liberating) mobility has resulted in the continuous traffic jam of the post-modern present. More seriously, and described extensively by Sloterdijk, is the way how scientific research of atomic energy has led to a series of disastrous accidents involving nuclear plants and a seemingly unsolvable waste problem. Likewise, there is the failed ambition to reshape international politics into a controllable order, one that might have prevented the continuing forced escalation of this moment.

12. <u>I b i d .</u>, p. 23
13. <u>I b i d .</u>

'Es kommt anders, als man denkt, weil man die Rechnung ohne die Bewegung gemacht hat', Sloterdijk says, and this conclusion on the ultimately disastrous workings of this kinetic mechanism also applies to the project of contemporary urban planning. That project was started as a far-ranging exercise in control, and it was closely linked to the architectural aesthetics of the historic avant-garde. This, however, did not lead to the 'garden city of tomorrow', or any of modern urban planning's other emblems, but instead to the rather amorphous reality of the dispersed city.

In Sloterdijk's analysis of the current human condition, humanity has had to pay for its assumed control with a newly acquired passivity, equal to that of pre-modern times. This passivity imports that we are subject to forces and powers that will prove to be untameable and will inevitably lead to our ruin. Others have voiced the same perspective, even someone like the hard-cord positivist and neo-Darwinist Daniel Dennett. In an interview for the Dutch newspaper N R C H a n d e l s b l a d he was questioned on his idea about the technology's development and volunteered a interesting anecdote: 'A few years ago, I attended a conference on cognitive robotics in England. To my great surprise the conference was sponsored by British Telecom. Why? Because that company has created this fantastic network that it has grown beyond the company's understanding. No one gets it anymore. No individual. No specialist team. So they wanted to see if it was possible to come up with a robot human enough to communicate with us and, at the same time, computer enough to understand the network. The fact they considered this an important enough subject to spend several days talking with us illustrates that one can get a very uneasy feeling about something one has invented but can no longer control. It's like riding an elephant and having no idea where it is heading. All they can do is hope that it doesn't crash into an abyss.' [14]

There does seem to be an abyss at the end, unless someone manages to get the elephant to stop. This grim culmination of what once began as a kinetic utopia seems to be announced today by a never-ending stream of

14. Bas Heijne, "Ooit willen we ook kunsthersenen": Daniel C. Dennett, Amerikaans filosoof over de biologische goocheldoos', in: N R C H a n d e l s b l a d (M-maandbijlage) (May 2005)

ecological, climatological, and political calamity. The time frame within which this conclusion will unfold is, however, still open-ended. It is remarkable that, after centuries of pathological mobility, the world order seems to be heading toward a phase of relative quiet, albeit a quietness caused by congestion and constraint.

The kinetic utopia, after all, has not produced an ever-smoother flow of traffic, but on the contrary, an ever-growing traffic jam; it has not guaranteed a constant supply of new energy but halting and hampering systems. Humankind has regressed to the passivity and dependency of its pre-modern condition. Indeed, we seem to be right back where we started from. And exactly because of these current blockades even Dennett's abyss may very well stay out of reach, not in the last place of destructive spirits – their ominous intentions have every chance of being smothered in traffic jams and other random inconveniences.

The diagnosis of stagnation caused by inertia, completed by universally looming perspectives, applies as much to the latest architecture and urban culture as it does to any other social phenomenon. What is more, the philosophical approach of the current human condition seems to present itself conspicuously in the theory and practice of the spatial order; in fact, it has been leaving its marks there ever since the middle of the twentieth century. But even socially committed architects of today, which includes Ton Venhoeven, have taken up Sloterdijk's pessimistic outlook on contemporary culture. Inspired by this, Venhoeven's architecture presents itself as a philosophically motivated spectacle. Subject of this spectacle is the unleashing kinetic utopia of late modernism. The stage for the spectacle is designed according to the principles of a cultural climate determined by the globalization issue. The idea Sloterdijk presents in his book Im Weltinnenraum des Kapitals, is that, after ages of exploration and conquest, the world has, in the final, electronic phase of globalization, reached a stage of distance no longer forming an obstacle, or, for those who perceived it as such, a challenge.[15] Around the year 1600, about half of the earth was familiar to the Europeans. Two hundred years later, four-fifths had been explored; another two centuries further the entire globe has become acutely accessible. 'Wenn die entdeckte Welt anfangs ins Unermeßliche zu wachsen

15. Peter Sloterdijk, Im Weltinnenraum des Kapitals (Frankfurt am Main: Suhrkamp, 2005)

26

schien schrumpft sie mit dem Abschluß des Zeitalters zu einem kleinen Ball, zu einem Punkt, zusammen', Sloterdijk concludes.[16]

Globalization's final destination is in fact no more than a dot, apparently representing a stagnating kinetic utopia. On closer inspection, however, this dot does appear to have a spatial manifestation, although it is referred to in somewhat vague terminology – at least for the time being. Sloterdijk identifies space in the completed stage of globalization as space turned inside out (the Weltinnernraum des Kapitals), metaphorically described as a 'greenhouse' that sucks in everything that was formerly looked for outside or in the distance.[17]

    This greenhouse is not an open-air market place, nor is it an agora: it is a consumer palace where costumers can make their choices in more or less controlled conditions.

Allusions about the further make-up of the Weltinnenraum makes it clear that this final stage of globalization is more likely to produce inertia and introspection than expansion.[18] A large part of this make-up consists of spatial complexes allotted with apartments, consistently called 'cells' by Sloterdijk. This term seems appropriate for the 'celibate ontology' of recent days, a concept referring to the way people live. Apartments are increasing structured into a coherent 'immune system' of individuals who live separately and maintain a closely programmed relationship with the outside world, unwilling to form communities in the traditional sense.

These conglomerate buildings of apartments, or cells, complemented by broadly programmed accommodations for work, and several collective facilities like stadiums, together define a contemporary city's major intrinsic and formal components. For the inhabitants of the city, its concrete overall shape is no longer of great importance, less so, in any way, than the mostly virtual networks that now characterize their lives.

Not only the city itself is confronted with this eroding significance of its

16. Ibid., p. 159

17. Ibid., p. 26

18. See the magazine Arch+ (2004, nr. 169/170), which was dedicated entirely to Sloterdijk.

material appearance; for a while now, architecture as a whole has been exposed to this process. The tendency to design buildings according to an archetypal grammar (based on the classical canon that was completed during the Renaissance) had all but disappeared during the heydays of Modernism, and had truly vanished after the World War II. Movement and instability had become the new themes, a development that unsettled architecture as such. Architects adapted accordingly by aiming to closely interweave design and landscape, according to De Solà-Morales, who summarized the tenor of the fifties in the words dematerialization, fragmentation, and camouflage.[19]

The tenor of the architecture from the fifties has only become stronger since then. Along the way, however, architectural designers did adjust their strategy to cope with their limited freedom. The pursuit of integration has made room for something different, says De Solà-Morales in a description that characterizes estrangement as typical of contemporary architecture: 'Contemporary architectures make their appearance ex abrupto, taking us by surprise. Their presence is not connected to a place. Our reception of them is almost always mediated or mediatized by photographic, video, and computerized images, by possible views, and by the disconnection between the built and what goes on around it.'

What used to be integration has become estrangement. But in both cases we are looking at architecture having to face the unleashed dynamics of urban life, while no longer having its foundation of an eternal grammar as Alberti's, for example. This is why De Solà-Morales considers integration and estrangement as being 'two faces of the same problematic coin'.[20]

It is precisely here, in this area of tension, where we can find the source of Ton Venhoeven's buildings. The classics have all died, for Venhoeven as well, but still there are inspiring ideas like Alberti's who plainly stated that 'a building is like an animal, the nature of which needs to be recreated.'[21]

19. De Solà-Morales 1999, pp. 20-21

20. Ibid., p. 21

21. Quoted from: Liane Lefaivre, Alexander Tzonis, De oorsprong van de moderne architectuur: een geschiedenis in documenten (Nijmegen: SUN, 1984), p. 67

Camouflage used to be applied in honour of architecture's naturalistic roots. Nowadays, it stems from the composition weakening the moment when building density and functional turnover of buildings increase to such an extent that traditional architecture loses its meaning.

The higher the level of congestion becomes, the more feverishly a building's function changes, the shorter its life-span, and the more fertile the ground for the formation of a landscape to replace a former city. Landscapes can accommodate changes of every complexity, without the burden of an architecture grammar handed down over generations.

In Venhoeven's PowerPoint presentation, therefore, natural forms, cities, and buildings act in concert; the same holds for his designs. The interaction between these worlds is electrifying. His buildings are set on a stage consisting of forms that are transient, such as events or machines, as opposed to the permanent structures of traditional architecture: they don't take root but instead are plugged in.

Globalization has created a universal hub, where the streets are coloured by the daily news brought in from elsewhere, an elsewhere that is now part of the very same hub: the news is just not what it used to be. As long as Sloterdijk's kinetic utopia has reached the phase of its inherent catastrophe, technological progress remains the driving force – until further notice. We can see this too in the evolution of Venhoeven's oeuvre. Buildings now turn the corner with perfect ease, made possible by a logic of production adapted for computer technology. Designing a building that not only seeks out the camouflaging landscape but also incorporates it, requires complicated processing of programme and composition. The order of interior spaces is no longer in line with Durand's common sense at the outset of the modern project. Far from it: it seems to conform only to nature's erratic ways. Designing a building that resembles an animal or a cave calls for extensive knowledge about stretching the skin over the building's skeleton, creating the right tactility and the right flowing lines.

This object, composed as it is of different worlds, convinces through its refinement of the unequal parts of the composition and the way the façade grips around the corner. Indeed, the object presents itself as an alien rather than a true product of nature, which is in line with De Solà-Morales' characterization. This could be mere habituation, after an unprepared leap into

29

the evolution of the building. One and a half decade ago, deconstructivism offered no more than an anecdotal overture to exploring a territory that no longer has any secrets. The activities in this territory now seem like an endgame with architecture ultimately the losing party. Or might there be, despite Sloterdijk's dark clouds, a new grammar emerging – perhaps as was the case when the primitive hut contained the seed of the Doric order? We don't know. And, with the passivity that, apparently, becomes us so well, we simply wait and see. The various scientific spheres that had been kept separate so carefully by the modernist project – the grand kinetic utopia – are short-circuiting and beginning to converge: nature inclines toward culture, and so the works of earth, sky, and water draw closer to the works of the mind.

We need to reconquer the evacuated space of representation
Wim Nijenhuis

'(...) the movement, in which the movement's very trace must be evident reveals itself by (...) détournement (...)' Guy Debord, <u>Society of the Spectacle</u> (1967)

With their extraordinarily fascinating architecture, VenhoevenCS stages a remarkable world of references. Side by side with the measureless techno-surface of the <u>Star Wars</u> 'Death Star', where the image of the planet merges with that of the machine, we find the immeasurable rock faces of the pueblos in Mesa Verde and the Canyon de Chelley. Mega-constructions featuring in science fiction are just as likely to inspire a shape or form, as is a prehistoric settlement – especially when a tear or other imperfection in the smooth surface reveals a glimpse of the complex interior. And then there are the animals – the fish, a herd, and the ray, hiding in the sand – fraternizing with technical equipment – the coachwork and the headlights of a car, the circuit board and the shell of a computer, the entrance to a comic-book spaceship. VenhoevenCS seems to imply that technical creations are kinds of animals, and vice versa. The Laboratory Building in Zwijndrecht however refers to a very special creature: the chimera – the multi-headed monster with a lion's head, a goat's head on its back, and occasionally portrayed with a serpent's head at the end of its tail. Throughout history, the chimera has become the icon of the hybrid and the quintessential symbol of chaos. Fantastic to the extreme, its name had soon become synonymous with 'phantasm', or 'illusion'.

The two kinds of references mentioned above seem to merge in two re-

31

markable examples of VenhoevenCS' oeuvre: the Jan Schaefer Bridge and the design for the Combination Building on the Cruquiusweg, both in Amsterdam. The merge here, so it seems, is for the purpose of an even greater mission: a reference to a world, be it the mythical world of the techno-monster, or, to put it more neutrally, that of the techno-being. We can see that VenhoevenCS' world is by no means limited by mere reality. On the contrary. Each one on its own or all of them mixed together, either directly or from a distance – these appearances provide the shapes that are moulded long enough for them to fit the desired function, the building regulations, and the building's specific situation, but always without explicitly expressing them.

Even though, at first sight, these mythical references seem to be applied without any preconceived system, they do serve the same function in all of VenhoevenCS' architecture: to reconquer the previously evacuated r e p r e s e n t a t i o n a l   s p a c e. They do so, not to create some fashionable identity, but rather to engage, from a hallucinatory approach, in an interplay with the radical illusion of the architectural object. The radical illusion is most unlike the banal illusion – charged as it is with negative implications of deceit and doomed from the beginning to be rectified. The radical illusion is characterized precisely by the radical impossibility of the object to exist in its very own presence, to be equal to itself, and to be real. In the same way that we do not experience the reality of a star but a mirage of its light hitting our retinas many of thousands of light-years afterwards, so it is with every object and every creature in the world. Nothing is identical to itself. Relationships between objects always embody a hiatus, a distortion, a gap, which excludes any reduction of the same to the same. For architectural objects, too, there is no escaping this gap that splits every object and every being in this world right in the heart of their existence. This gap defeats any rectification of the representation. Its existence signs the death warrant of the terror of fact. Rather than seeing that as a loss, this is an opportunity that is accepted by VenhoevenCS with great enthusiasm.

Ever since the avant-garde movement of the twentieth century, architecture, in desperate attempt to rescue its 'meaning', has engaged in a sinister relationship with the advertising and media world, resulting in a ferocious attack on the sign. Step by step, architecture has been corrupted by the information economy and by its pursuit of its typical capital: the accumulated attention. The aim was to increase 'public visibility', on the one hand, by bringing the closed formation of the object sign of design, which was meant to publicize itself, on the other hand, by promoting the activities of the architects themselves. In order to bring themselves closer to 'politics', architects like Gropius, Meier, and Costa had themselves appointed directors of design academies. Le Corbusier and Mies van der Rohe, for example, increased their visibility by taking radical positions, organizing exhibitions, publishing magazines, and writing manifests. This trend came to a temporary end with the strategy of the 'identifiable object', which inspired Frank Gehry for his Guggenheim Museum in Bilbao. Here, everything is focused on creating presence.

Architecture's c o r r u p t i o is closely connected with the blackmail by the 'logic of the surface' and its mysterious potential to challenge and reverse the structure of the object sign. Industrial products and architectural objects are characterized by a complex semiotic structure consisting of material, form, and meaning. This tripartite structure inspires different experiences and prevents the object sign to freeze into a set identity. There is always some remainder, uncontrollable and open to experience, that escapes the control of the form that provides it its meaning. When 'presence' is sought through the media and via publicity, then the 'logic of the surface' requires a 'representation' of the architectural project in a format that suits information technology. To be able to be printed in magazine and displayed on computer screens, an architectural project has to be without remainder so it can be compressed into a two-dimensional image of itself. All information is channelled onto an extensive and synthetic surface – designed for quick perception and flexible reception – that imposes a set identity on the representation.

It is for this reason that information is always aesthetically designed. It is a 'form' of which perceptibility and immediate readability, not meaning, are the main functions. The more the amount of information that circulates in the media and becomes available in the metropolis' public spaces increases, the more the rule of perceptibility demands from this information to be targeted towards the attention of a potential observer. Under pressure from an ever-increasing information surplus, a scarcity of attention dictates the aesthetic rule of form. As aesthetics take the forefront in information design, the traditional division of labour between architecture, the arts, and the realm of products (as still existed at the onset of the industrial era) becomes obsolete.

With the fusion of architecture, art, advertising, and industry in the early twentieth century, it seemed, for a brief moment, that avant-garde architecture and art had cut the 'chains of appearance', which tied them to monumental buildings and museums. This situation had, until then, reduced their functioning to the 'display of incapacity' of the symbolic act. So, for a moment it seemed as if this fusion made it possible to absorb the metropolitan reality in a now effective 'art trade'. In that sense, the transgression of architecture and art outside their institutional limits, and their murder of the sign seemed to be a positive response to the modern question 'whether and how activities of an aesthetic character, whether and how art is able "to give shape to history"' [22]

But what if we look at the above process from the opposite perspective? Then we see how the metropolitan world of goods, market, publicity, and even of the academies and architecture practice has stripped architecture – through the advance of technical visual media and other communication techniques – right from the start of its exclusive position as producer of objects that call for our attention. In the nineteen thirties (the era of the grand cinemas) the architecture of the monument, of the palaces, the churches, markets, hospitals, and theatres had to start sharing its position within the so called attention economy with the movies and with photography, with industrial design and advertising, and later, with television. This competition has compelled architecture to closely guard its position in the public sphere and to experiment with new strategies for capturing the attention. Out in the open and unshielded public space of the metropolis, bombarded with and complemented by the co-extensive 'public space' of the media and networks, architecture is constantly at risk of being overtaken by new developments in the race for attention – only to sink back into social insignificance. Oddly enough, it is the remnants of the institutional sphere of the discipline, and sometimes that of museums, that manage to re-integrate architecture into the business of art and science.

22. Martin Heidegger, Nietzsche I (1961) Nietzsche: Volumes One and Two Harper One; New Ed. edition (March 1, 1991)

Right from the time it became a conscious practice, the art of staging attention was commissioned to the 'techniques of poor pretence'. Consciousness and theory of the 'economy of attention' were developed in propaganda, fashion, and, eventually, advertising. Politically correct cultural criticism never got tired of countering this acquired knowledge with everything that required deep contemplation and accurate perception. Attention is primarily about how we spend our time. Only when our eyes are allowed enough time to slowly oscillate across an object or to scan a certain space, only then can an 'original perception' occur and does an' intuition based reflection' have a chance.[23] Anything faster than that inevitably turns us into 're-viewers' by forcing us to exploit our memories. In this manner the rule of advertising prescribes that the architectural representation has to offer the audience the opportunity to agree with a phantasmic dimension that already existed before and thus to associate the representation with the 'inner landscape' of their desires.

The corrupted strategy to 'save' architecture and its influence on society is falling prey to a fatal reversal brought about by the unfathomable irony of a mass audience – they see the already eroded representation as a 'presentation' and take this to be the actual object. In turn, the architectural object is itself becoming a sign of its presence in the media. The excess in 'saving', dictated by technology (photo, film, television, computer) has resulted in the post-modern 'substitution' of signs for the objects to which they refer. This process embodies the tragic variation on Hölderlin's famous quote, 'Where danger is, grows the saving power also', fitting so well the current situation if we reverse it: The more the saving power increases, the more danger there is.

'Ideological facts were never a simple chimaera, but rather a deformed consciousness of realities, and in this form they have been real factors which set in motion real deforming acts; all the more so when the materialization, in the form of spectacle, of the ideology brought about by the concrete success of autonomized economic production in practice confounds social reality with an ideology which has tailored all reality in terms of its model. Ideology is the abstract will to universality and the illusion as-

23. Paul Virilio, The Aesthetics of Disappearance, tr. P. Beitchman (New York: Semiotext(e), 1991)

sociated with that will. (...) At this point, ideological pretention acquires a sort of flat positivistic exactitude.'[24] Here we find a hint as to the second attack on the space of representation: that of the scientific and social motivation of the sign. Analogue to scientific discourse, architecture should follow the habitus of the art of engineering and join its pursuance of 'the true form'.

In my dissertation Een wolk van duister weten (A Cloud of Dark Knowledge), published in 2003, I discuss how the ascendance of Simon Stevin – the unrelenting enemy of even the slightest notion of a 'Gaya Scienza' – towards the end of the Renaissance marks the onset within the world of engineering and scientific architecture of a quest for 'reliable knowledge'. This reliability is based on the unequivocally motivated correspondence between sign and reality, word and object, representation and referent, and forms the heart of the exact scientific approach that has plagued our universities even till today. No doubt, the reliability of the signs of our communication are the principal rule in scientific information. Stevin attacked the Renaissance 'epistèmè of resemblances' (Foucault) with accusations of 'deception' and 'simulation ', a clear indication that the propagation of the 'reliable' sign was needed to justify the status of a 'theoretical practice' that could exist independently of the realm of 'experience'. 'When therefore theorists lacking practical knowledge, like Ptolemy, Euclid, Vitrivius, and their equals were, restrict themselves to theory, then they practise their profession irreproachable'[25] Stevin openly opposed the 'false notion' that was always possible in a scientific discourse and an artistic practice that, on the one hand, promoted resemblance and expressiveness, and, on the other hand, assumed material experience. Stevin (and all those others who shared the same discursive formation) built their power of expertise on postulating the possibility of a reliable enunciation (statement). In order to obtain more influence, professionals had to become experts by applying a new definition of truth. He countered the Renaissance preference for prob-

24. Guy Debord, Society of the Spectacle (1967), http://www.marxists. org/reference/archive/debord/society.htm
25. Simon Stevin, Burgherlick Leven & anhangh (1590), Het burgherlick leven & anhangh/Simon Stevin, Pim den Boer (ed.) (Utrecht: Bijleveld, 2001)

ability with the idea of 'validity' of a statement. Against the Renaissance thinkers and artists unwilling to let go of the interchange of resemblance, Stevin motivated the valid sign with the productive effect it was to have 'in the long run'.

This 'long run' never hesitated to produce the irrational phenomenon of the fatal curving of time and the fall of history into its present catastrophic situation/condition. Today, precisely those who tenaciously hold on to the principle of reliability are the ones who burden us with counterproductive effects of insignificant facts and bits of information that accumulate to an excess of positivism, an excess of information.

The power of the theoretical expert is all about the style of the expression. This is why Stevin opted for heavily regulated language and equally regulated design. Stevin suggested we should limit ourselves to statements about the dimensions of things. An enunciation like 'this table is three metres long' refers to a concrete table and says something about its characteristics. One can verify the statement simply by measuring the actual table.

Stevin tried to implement these ideas in his designs for the ideal city and his encampments, described in his work Vande oirdeningh der steden (On the Order of Cities), published in 1599. Regular divisions and geometrical forms like the square being grouped together in countable series were used to enable the creation of well-organized compositions that could be known immanently, that is, without having to revert to external forms. In contrast, Stevin's opponents often based their design of buildings and cities on the resemblance with the human body in order to define in which way the form they had put together was 'integral'.

Even though Stevin formulated his theories in the period of Mannerism, when representation ruled in the arts and sciences, he was at the same time looking to eliminate representation in favour of direct reference to the reality and revelation of an object's characteristics, excluding the influence of experience. Stevin's contemporaries noted that he wasn't always clear in distinguishing between the definition of words and the definition of objects, and that he enforced their correspondence by reverting to moral and religious categories like 'betrayal' and 'conscience'.

There is, however, a remarkable parallel between the 'anatomical lesson' in medical science, Stevin's ideal of direct reference, and, in our days, the television reporting on disaster and war: the murder of the symbolic dimension of the sign actually goes hand in hand with the repression of sympathy, that extraordinary, touching resemblance that, 'by drawing things towards one another in an exterior and visible motion, also gives rise to a hidden interior motion'.[26] It goes without saying that the paradigm of the 'reliable form' and the 'immanence of the sign' determined the habitus of the Modernist movement, at the same time trying to capture the meaning of the form into a binding relationship with the construction's function with the intention of guaranteeing 'sincerity'.

From the nineteen sixties onwards, attempts were made to turn architectural representations into 'truth' by infusing them with the creative energy of the social. In fact, the 'open planning process', the 'open design process', the hearings and the participation procedures were no more than scenarios to guarantee 'truth in form' by compensating for the ever-present 'communication deficiency'. Later on, this deficiency was exposed as the nihilism of the masses, produced by the media themselves.

The corruption of architecture by the information industry, as mentioned above, has reinforced the totalitarianism of 'credulity'. This is why most architects refrain from checking this nihilism disseminated by the mass media; rather, they assume that obscenity of the techniques of presentation will simply go on. Much of today's aesthetics (their performance taken from the media and based on the logic of the surface) is characterized by an ever-disappointing reticence that eventually strives to abolish the contemplative observer altogether.

In essence, this corrupting process is fed by contempt and the success of this contempt. Experts in reticent aesthetics (who never allow a reciprocal answer, only coded responses) are repeatedly confirmed in their contempt by the knowledge they have of contemptible men, what they consider the observer to be. For this alone VenhoevenCS deserves our sympathy: against the current trend, they opt to reconquer representation and, in doing so, create new opportunities for sympathy.

26. Michel Foucault, The Order of Things (New York: Vintage Books, 1994 (1970))

'The "new power of fraud," (…) must be understood as a systematic organization of the "failure of the faculty of encounter" and as its replacement by a social h a l l u c i n a t o r y fact.'[27]

Debord supposed that our culture was frozen in a 'refusal of history', but also that history works/operates underneath like some creative energy that propels that society forward in a direction in which ideology and culture would dissolve, taking with them their media and producers, including architecture. The result of this would be a 'de-alienation': a sudden plunge of the (historical) subject that had been doomed to inertia into the reality of a re-liquefied history and who thus would regain its sovereignty. The architecture of the sixties and seventies had taken an option on this development, assuming that their procedures would stimulate the rehabilitation of reality.

VenhoevenCS realizes that this notion has been superseded by a new situation. Beyond history's critical state, a state in which criticism and crisis still had a role to play, we have skidded into the catastrophic state of history in which the accidental has become general. Architecture is no longer moved by a motion that, in the long run, would link it up with reality, but by the systematic intrusion of something deviating that functions according to certain incomprehensible rules. This is why VenhoevenCS – just like all great thinkers and artists of Mannerism – accepts that it would be impossible and immoral to create the illusion the image could be controlled by linking it to truth or reality, or that it would be better to abandon it completely like Debord in his M o v i e   W i t h o u t   I m a g e s from 1952. The idea that 'ornament is crime' is opposed by the idea that the image is neither restrained by truth, nor by reality because the image is something from beyond, to which it is bound. It is part of a mystery, of the 'illusion of the world'. Like the illusion, the image prevents a truth based on certainty from emerging, and prevents reality being taken as something certain. Its obstruction of certainty is not a weakness; it is a strength that correctly corresponds to the catastrophic state of history.

Portrait paintings or poems, on the other hand, are 'remote signs': these are not direct references but present the truth in a way that is associated

27. Guy Debord, S o c i e t y   o f   t h e   S p e c t a c l e (1967), h t t p : / / w w w . m a r x i s t s . o r g / r e f e r e n c e / a r c h i v e / d e b o r d / s o c i e t y . h t m

with an experience. The distance between sign and referent is the playing field of an intelligence that we might call 'poetic'. It departs from the idea of 'intuitive understanding', this slightest inceptive moment in the soul that occurs before the seeds of the known and the unknown intertwine and crystallize into a concept. This extraordinary experience of understanding happens somewhere in between the individual's perception and that which is perceived, or, phrasing it in a somewhat more radical way: between the unwary/innocent subject and the surprise power of the 'objectile'. When we are touched by something it is these tiniest inceptive moments in our soul, these 'moments of intuition and imagination' that unfold new worlds and that evoke in us a sympathetic passion. Compared to this 'practical power' of representation, the 'direct and certain reference' of information is nothing more than a banal implosion of the space of representation that crushes the living experience and squeezes it to death.

The image endorses life because it knows it must dance with its subject; it also knows this dance sometimes becomes a wrestle. Representation implies that the image respects its subject and maintains a distance between them without aspiring to any form of identity or fusion. After all, when we dance or wrestle we don't mean to merge with our partner and become the same. We stay who we are and our time together is based on a silent pact that respects the distance between us. In this way, the superior figure of regulative fiction rises from the ashes of the valid concordance. It would be a mistake to think the space of representation is the portal of sternness and importance, and should be pushed aside in favour of montage, which, supposedly, is more adept at expressing the complexity of the metropolitan reality than the 'historical style'. Representation is neither expression nor communication. The image often serves to describe something, to show something, and to mean something; yet it also exists as a poetic form. In that case it is a material presence as well as a deviation, an element from beyond, the magic of which correlates with an unfathomable absence.

Through the visual references in their architecture VenhoevenCS wants to break a lance for illusion and magic. By taking up position beyond the truth and by taking a hallucinatory point of view, they cunningly counter the current norms of representation as well as every principle of truth and cause. For what purpose? The power of the mythical image exists in its deviation and its capacity to r e d u c e a complex reality. This is why it fits so well into the order of disappearances.

'Amidst the clamour of the metropolis the image can once again introduce silence and emptiness.'

The rehabilitation of metaphor

The space of representation arises there where the sign acquires independence. Representation existed in medieval and Renaissance times but relied upon the resemblance of one natural form and another (as was common in medicine) or of a transcendental reality with a contingent one (as in architecture and urban planning). These resemblances could involve reduction. It was not always necessary for the models that were actualized in the representation to be reproduced in their entirety. A part could easily represent the whole. This confidence in the principle of metonymy served as the bases for the reduction of the prototype to some of its characteristics. The uttering of 'Urbs beata Jerusalem' (Blessed Jerusalem) made the place where it was spoken into a true Temple of Jerusalem. The square layout of the city, or merely a few columns in the church, could generate a similar effect. The metaphor may have been selective but never arbitrary in its choice, even though sometimes it is hard to decipher. VenhoevenCS' architecture is not primarily focussed on resemblance, but on metaphor as an independent variable. The decisive criteria are the independent and arbitrary qualities of the sign. Other than during the Renaissance, with its well-known correspondence of the macro- and microcosm, in the classicist era the sign was staged as an independent variable with its own material presence. This enabled it to offer other options than the knowledge of a divine truth, or to fathom the essence of a certain case. Through its own material existence the independent sign affects impressions and brings about instinctive reactions which, in turn, can be recalled when prompted by the sign. At the same time, it combines memories from elsewhere with its referent. The space of representation pulls the sign off its double moorings: that of the divine word and that of nature. It places the representation in its surroundings and recognizes its independent identity. Now, the sign has the power to 'connect'. It connects the idea of something with the idea of

41

something else. It now envelops two ideas: that of the actual representation and that of what is represented. The nature of the free and independent sign of representation consists in evoking the former through the latter; however, it also has the power to create conflict between them.

The headway VenhoevenCS has made in the reconquering of the space of representation and the rehabilitation of metaphor has fostered the power of a 'true art of reduction' and the creation of room for a 'style that contains its own criticism'. Beyond the shallow positivism of the media, modern architecture, and the 'museumizing' ossification of culture in general, they demand mobility through images in which traces of motion can still be perceived. Evidently, the space of representation is a precondition for a form of architecture that wants, by incorporating the traces of the motion it makes into the representation, to make the mobility of sign and meaning part of the experience. The exemplary 'détournement' of images from other fields is characteristic of VenhoevenCS's 'rebellious style', a style that barrages the increasing strangeness of architecture with an architecture of the strangeness. Kierkegaard stated that blending familiar and unfamiliar elements 'confuses by the memories this evokes'.[28] The gesture of détournement re-establishes the subversive character of those cultural elements that have fossilized into 'venerable monuments'.

The foremost principle of the 'rebellious style' is therefore to maintain a distance from all that is coagulated into officially accepted truths and codified styles. There is the implicit invitation to despise those who despise the observer, and who are constantly reconfirmed in their contempt by their 'knowledge of the contemptible being' that the observer actually is in their eyes. In our catastrophic state of history, the 'rebellious style' wants to shift, little by little, the coagulated truth and its ossified elements and so help us to gradually work our way out of their hold. In the process, it sets in motion 'a practical force' that opens the way from contempt and indifference to sympathy and compassion.

28. Wijsgerige Kruimels (1955). Søren Kierkegaard, Philosophical Fragments or A Fragment of Philosophy by Johannes Climacus, published by S. Kierkegaard, Kierkegaard's Writings, Volume 7, edited by Edna H. Hong; Howard V. Hong (Princeton, N.J.: Princeton University Press, 1985)

For VenhoevenCS, metaphors are the ultimate way to protest today's aesthetic nihilism as is expressed in the recycling of historical forms in postmodernism and the constantly failing canonising of modern architecture by those eager to turn it into some kind of contemporary classicism. Developments over the past few decades have made one thing clear: normative classicism is not an option. This will always lead to short-lived, artificial constructions in which tectonics itself becomes ornamental and in which style fails to escape the grips of fashion.

Metamorphosis is Baroque's rule. It is the 'art of change' that carries the principle of transience in its heart and recognizes it also in the world. Theatre and feast, theatrical feast, and festive theatre continuously refer to the décor of the constructed place through a construction entirely devoted to 'transition'. In a delicate balance it is inscribed in the stormy foundation of 'Physis' with its power to give or take as it pleases. All of the relativism of this 'art of change' is dedicated to the bidding of life against eternity.

The architectural design practice has completely lost this baroque concept of the 'whole'. We do, however, find traces of this in the contemporary 'consumption' of architecture as a whole, in both a historical and geographical sense. The collection of architecture from all over the world and from every time in history allocates each architectural articulation a relative value within a general and interactive 'disorder' which is erected as a baroque structure on a higher plane. Not a single expression can escape its fate of being absorbed by this chaotic, abstract building, this 'museumizing solidification'. Through the media's publicity we can now become familiar with and accept the architecture of every time and every place. The 'collection of memories', on display in the instable museum of the media has set off a process which will eventually lead to the end of the enclosed 'world of architecture' because it destroys the very foundations of its ability to engage into a meaningful communication with its audience.

That is why the mythical architecture of motility and the calculating interaction with change (which doesn't hesitate to assign the image the part of the immobile mask that masks any change) is so characteristic of the era of the disintegration of discipline. At the same time it embodies the architecture that will survive this disintegration because it is part of a living cul-

43

ture. By the way, it happens to be at its most 'avant-garde' as it puts itself at risk and expresses the 'impossibility of change'.

A metaphor can summarize a complex spatial reality for the senses and can offer a definition of this that is not restricted by the singular architectural object or by the idea of the building. In VenhoevenCS' designs we see constellations in which the metaphor of the 'herd' comprises a city district, such as the design for the Dongezone in Tilburg, or that a building is seriously deconstructed, as is the case with the day care centre in Soest. In the latter building, the play with the different qualities of the building has become the actual subject of the architecture – fully in line by the way with the 'rebellious style' of Karl Marx. Outside has become inside, the facade is positioned in the heart of the building, constructions usually meant to cover and conceal now do the opposite, the layout is obscure and even involves vertical aspects, and so forth. The metaphor also lends a binding principle to a complex of spaces that disappear from the landscape, are concealed underneath a clever 'camouflage net', but still remain coherent thanks to the metaphor of the 'being', like the ray in the case of the Jan van Galenbad swimming pool in Amsterdam.

Through its distance, the space of representation gives architectural design the ability to counter the solidified truth of the building in the name of higher cultural principles: a creativity of 'self change' which is receptive to the experience of 'transgression ' without a compulsive need to actually cross boundaries, all this completed by an ethical self control that cherishes a certain level of suspicion towards a fixed identity that might become too flat.

The rule of things

'In our media-dominated world, concrete objects have automatically become master of our social life.' [29]
    We should ask ourselves if we should, like Debord, take this situation pejoratively as the 'new power of fraud'. There is no denying, however, that it is rooted in a technology and production where 'the new domain of

29. Guy Debord, Society of the Spectacle (1967), http://www.marxists. org/reference/archive/debord/society.htm

44

alien beings to whom man is subservient... grows coextensively with the mass of objects.' This brings us to the situation in which the dominant factor is 'the life of what is dead, moving within itself.' (Hegel).

In his book An der Zeitmauer (1959) (At the Wall of Time) the German expressionist Ernst Jünger postulates the concept of a point beyond the plan, where any supply of energy increases calamity and where it is better not to act than to act. When in the middle of the era of the plan, the catastrophic state of history makes its entry and we yield to the 'power of the gods', and 'the darker side of fate' seems stronger than our plans, then what is the secret that lies therein? Technical and scientific inventions and concoctions are spinning their web around us while 'science beyond the molecule' demonstrates clearly that 'the universe is alive'. Not only do we constantly respond to the Objektbefehl from machines and appliances, we also enter into situations in which objects address us directly and autonomously, like the noise on the radio, the crackling on the telephone, a sudden wrong connection, or whatever early onset of artificial intelligence. According to Jünger, these are not revelations of 'technology', that is always linked to the perseverance of the human will, but manifestations of the 'intrusive'. The 'Spirit of History', or the 'creative energy', which burdens us with the delusion of being the only and lonely form of intelligence within the cosmos, is approached from beyond by matter that strives to assume an 'intelligence' of its own and doesn't hesitate to surreptitiously use human inventions to further its cause.

Is it enough to characterize VenhoevenCS' architecture as 'fascinistic', and to say it 'plays with the unusual'? Are they concerned with the 'confrontation of form' and the 'estrangement of the semiotic sign in view of its content'? I think so, but I also think this is overshadowed by their radicalization of dialectics. Through their designs, VenhoevenCS seems to communicate to us that a creative principle must be attributed not only to the spirit, but also to objects. On closer inspection, the passive role that was assigned to objects as well as animals by antiquity (when matter was considered subordinate to the spirit) appears to have been a rather awkward makeshift solution. The old gnostic myths essentially accept that matter is eternally autonomous and has its own creative power, which manifests itself in superior inviolability, sudden interruptions, accidents, coincidences, seductions, and mysterious manipulations, all of which find

45

their origin in the realm of concrete objects. VenhoevenCS recognizes this and have therefore abandoned the idealistic position that always stresses the sovereignty of humankind.

'Reason must approach nature with its principles … [and] be instructed by it not like a pupil, who has recited to him whatever the teacher wants to say, but like an appointed judge who compels witnesses to answer the questions he puts to them.' [30] If they were to follow Kant, this might result in matter, restricted by their power of judgement, and thus reacquiring again a meaning that derives from a higher principle.

Sovereign matter, on the other hand, is external and foreign to the creative subject and its ideas, and 'refuses to allow itself to be reduced to one solely principled by the great ontological machines.' [31]

To conceive of the new metaphysical unity of man and machine, Ernst Jünger introduced the notion of the 'organic construction'. The International Situationists saw the world as being ruled by objects: design objects and human objects. Hidden behind this was the plan and deception of the bourgeoisie. Fashion could be interpreted as a fatal response of objects to objects and the media has familiarized us with the obtrusiveness of the 'objectile'. To this series, VenhoevenCS adds the idea of the thing and the animal as the animated and eternal 'other' of the subject. Their 'magic animism' wants to do justice to a world that follows its own rules: a world we shall never understand, a world we cannot appropriate. A world, in short, both too vague and too poetically flamboyant.

30. Immanuel Kant, Critique of Pure Reason (1781), tr. Paul Guyer & Allan W. Wood (Cambridge/New York: Cambridge University Press, 1998)

31. Georges Bataille, 'Base Materialism and Gnosticism' (1930) in: Visions of Excess: Selected Writings (1927-1939) (Minneapolis: University of Minnesota Press, 1985)

What does it all mean?
Reflections on the work of VenhoevenCS
Pnina Avidar and Marc Schoonderbeek

Take 1. The edge of no control

'I would like to look at the world as one looks at a collection of postcards.'
-Evita Perón [32]

A picture on a postcard can be subject to many interpretations. There are at least three different stories a postcard tells us: a story about a certain place and the world, a story about the sender, and a story about the recipient. The represented, say, the image of the pyramids in Egypt could tell us about a great technological achievement, or about death rituals, or the story of slavery. A postcard is in fact a key to a whole world: it opens up the world of the sender, the recipient, the maker of the postcard; but also of the designer of what is depicted on the postcard.

A postcard (the 'poor man's telegraph') combines image, message, and factual information about a place. Starting a collection of postcards testifies of a desire to gain knowledge and understanding of the world. The communicative function of these 'story telling' images, constructs an extremely personal world-view. Since one can conceive many stories in relation to an image, a postcard offers a possible explanation of the world. You could say that Evita Perón saw the world as collectible, as a series of images that offer instant insight into the world.

32. Liliane Ruth Feierstein, 'The World as a Collection of Postcards; Evita's Architecture Project(ion)s in the Making of Argentinean Identity', conference proceedings Architecture and Identity (Berlin: 2004)

In this story, the represented architecture frames life. It embraces the sublime, the banal, and the grotesque. It creates room, in both a figurative and a literal sense, offers a stage and is the setting for every moment and events of life, from its inception till its end. It describes and inscribes the spatial conditions for an endless range of phenomena and needs: 'Architecture is defined by the actions it witnesses as much as by the enclosure of its walls. Murder in the Street differs from Murder in the Cathedral in the same way as love in the street differs from the Street of Love. Radically.'[33]

Architecture discerns both physical and metaphysical dimensions. Perhaps the sheer endlessness of these dimensions makes it impossible to grasp its full nature. Every attempt that is made to define architecture is faced with limitations and restrictions. The architectural 'being' proves impossible to identify. In line with the 'Aleph' by Borges[34] one can say that there is no solution to this 'central problem' of architecture, that is the enumeration (if only partially) of an infinitely complex whole. This could be the reason for the numerous variations in the discourse on architecture. Around every architectural object, a multitude of stories can unfold. This, wealth in narrative, has turned architecture into a literary discipline. As a literary category, the history of architecture is at least as fascinating as its core activity – construction. The narration previews all the possible daily activities that can be experienced in a virtual space. It is for this reason that Foucault spoke of an endlessly mirror construction 'erected against the black wall of death' that is 'fundamental for any language from the moment it determines to leave a trace of its passage.'[35]

Foucault considers narration an essential yet temporary suspension of death: 'its mirrored reflection upon death and the construction, from this reflection, of a virtual space where speech discovers the endless

33. Bernard Tschumi, The Manhattan Transcripts (London: Academy Editions, 1981/1994)

34. Jorge Luis Borges, De Aleph en andere verhalen (Amsterdam: De Bezige Bij, 1998) p. 426 (original: El Aleph (1949))

35. Michel Foucault, 'Language to Infinity', in: Language, Counter-Memory, Practice: Selected Essays and Interviews, tr. Donald F. Bouchard and Sherry, Donald F. Bouchard Simon (ed.) (Ithaca: Cornell UP, 1977), p. 55 (original: Le langage à l'infini (1963))

resourcefulness of its own image and where it can represent itself as already existing behind herself, already active beyond itself, to infinity.'[36]

Is architecture's unfeasible task then the creation of these spaces for which there is in fact no room? While Mies van der Rohe merely proposed architecture as the 'spatial expression of spiritual involvement'[37], this aching for the construction of the impossible place can have a paralysing effect. This is, however, a different form of paralysis than that of the emptiness reflected in most of today's architecture production. Neither the stilled silence of neo-minimalism (a direct result of the loss of certainties) nor the sublime futility Tafuri[38] describes, that no longer even tries to conceal the human impotence and nihilism, are prone to cultivate this impossible desire. Rather, this paralysis may be regarded as liberating when we consider projects that find an alternative approach to architecture in a conscientious exploration of chaos, in cultivating impotence, and in creating the architectural language to achieve these goals.

The designs of VenhoevenCS, the subject of this story, possess a remarkable quality, namely the creation of an almost hermetical closed world. They provide a spatial system that accommodates, supports and lets life run its course. Like immense 'mother ships' in space, or 'life laboratories', always ready to offer alienation and consolation. They distance themselves from their surroundings while their projection remains set on your retina. These are designs that illustrate the relationship between architecture and identity. They form the subject of a postcard that communicates a place's identity by means of an image.

Take 2. The key and the threshold

'I like architecture mythic, enigmatic, oblique and encrusted with decoration. I like it to suggest worlds, essences and supernatures. I despise the

36. Ibid., p. 9

37. For various descriptions and definitions of architecture by Mies, see: Fritz Neumeyer, Mies van der Rohe: Das kunstlose Wort (Berlin: Siedler, 1986), pp. 297-401

38. Manfredo Tafuri, Architecture and Utopia: Design and Capitalist Development (Cambridge/London: MIT Press 1976), p. 181

white, the simple and the tediously functional. I cannot bear the self-right-eous minimalist or the cynical post-modern ironicist. My preferred histori-cal architectural styles are the Baroque, Art Nouveau and the Gothic. ... These are styles and aspirations that seek to imbue architecture with the organic, the natural and the vital.' -Neil Spiller[39]

In the first chapter of The Ten Books on Architecture Marcus Vitruvius describes the range of architecture as a discipline. He begins with the architect's training, saying that an architect needs to gain broad knowledge of both the theory and practice of the field. 'In all matters, but particularly in architecture, there are these two points: – the thing sig-nified, and that which gives it significance.'[40] The object is the sign and the theory (in his case, scientific theory) lends meaning. The architect needs to speak in many 'languages'. The knowledge and understanding of a great variety of subjects, ranging from the arts to science, and from sociology to economics, form the tools to craft the signifying object. The object is then merely a reflection of the aggregate of existing knowl-edge and insights. Architecture is part of a cultural context, this complex of human patterns of knowledge, beliefs, language, and behaviour that are all dependent on the human capacity to communicate and transfer knowledge.

Culture, (or cultura in Latin, from the word colere meaning 'to work the land', 'to take care of', 'to nurture', 'to honour') involves a set of com-mon attitudes, values, and goals. Culture also represents the practice of forms of expression that characterize a group. Culture acts as a mediator by connecting individuals and groups with institutionalized hierarchies; in this respect it embodies relationships of power.

   Identity (from the Middle French identité, and the Late Latin identitat-, identitas, propably a contraction of the Latin identi-dem, in turn a combinations of idem et idem, literally meaning 'same and same') suggests equality that is having the essential or generic char-acteristics at different moments in time. From this perspective, architec-

39. Neil Spiller, 'Maverick Deviations', in: Neil Spiller, Lost Architectures (Chichester, West Sussex: Wiley-Academy, 2001), pp. 34-35
40. Marcus Vitruvius, The Ten Books on Architecture (New York: Dover Publications, 1960) p. 5

ture is a system of symbols that communicates cultural identity (the common similarity) through spaces and the envisioning of these spaces. The architectural space, which defines the p l a c e, is essential for the manifestation of a cultural identity.

VenhoevenCS' architectural narratives and representations exude a fascination with a seemingly uncontrolled ordering of the place. The underlying principles of this ordering process may not be immediately obvious from a visual point of view. They can, however, be clearly grasped through other sensory experiences, or cultural traditions. What we see here is the applying of order to a place and its direct surroundings by means of apparent disorder: a light touch of order, informal, convenient, full of surprising encounters and spatial convergences. Clearly not the formal order of a controlled garden, nor the rampant disorder of a garden neglected and untended. And also not the unrestrained wilderness of nature beyond human control. It is an order pushed over the limits of clarity, subject indeed to a certain level of neglect, but at the same time utilizing the historical import of the deformed remains of subtle shapes and colours of decline. It is the space of deformed fragments that enable, in their contorted effort of simulating coherence, the individuality of the place, of the encounter, of the personal identity. Is this the space where vulnerability rules?

The concept of 'place' involves more than merely the territorial limits of an area. 'A place is not just the where of something; it is location plus everything that occupies that location seen as an integrated meaningful phenomenon.'[41] Place is the synthesis of both natural and artificial objects, activities, function, and of the meaning it acquires from the various intentions. These components form a place's identity without, however, defining it. According to Edward Relph it is 'a special quality of insideness and the experience of being inside that sets places apart in space.'[42]

Carmen Popescu identifies three identification patterns in architecture and relates these to three concepts: place, history, and geography.[43]

41. Edward C. Relph, P l a c e a n d P l a c e l e s s n e s s (London: Pion, 1976), p. 3

42. I b i d ., p. 141

43. Carmen Popescu, 'Linking Notions: A Reconstructed Perspective of Identity and Architecture', conference proceedings A r c h i t e c t u r e a n d I d e n t i t y (Berlin: 2004)

Popescu believes that identity entered architectural thought as a determining concept around the beginning of the modern age (the nineteenth century) when the historical perspective was introduced through the philosophy of Hegel. Supposing that modern thought emphasizes the ongoing rationalization of society, then the notion of place (which can be strictly concrete as well as strictly abstract) remains the result of the development of scientific methods, tools, and techniques. The onset of the crisis of the modern project also signalled the start of a reinterpretation of the discipline's history. This 'reading' looks for differences (la différence) in knowledge, text, and sign. This crisis in modern thought has caused the identity to shatter, thus creating an endless number of differences and, at the same time, putting Place in a central position.

The architecture of this place, the focus of this essay, defines and creates these places through a specific space. This space then generates a specific identity that it communicates to others. This remarkable capacity to find a different language for every situation is a hallmark of this work. 'When I use a word', Humpty Dumpty said in rather a scornful tone, 'it means just what I choose it to mean – neither more or less.' 'The question is', said Alice, 'whether you can make words mean so many things'.[44] When language has been shattered into an endless number of fragments, when the word in fact undermines language itself and creates a 'profound fracture', then the various meanings of the object engulf the concept like an avalanche. When words can mean so many different things, do they then have any meaning at all?

Take 3. The utterer: no words necessary

'The Enlightenment dream of rational and transparent space, as inherited by modernist utopianism, was troubled from the outset by the realization that space as such was posited on the basis of an aesthetics of uncertainty and movement and a psychology of anxiety, whether nostalgically melancholic or progressively anticipatory.'[45] – Anthony Vidler

44. Lewis Carroll, Through the Looking Glass, Chapter VI (1872/1962)
45. Anthony Vidler, Warped Space; Art, Architecture, and Anxiety in Modern Culture (Cambridge/London: MIT Press, 2000), p. 3

The meaning inherent to the architectural object has thus been set in motion. The ensuing design strategy is aiming at the prolongation of this state. Allowing this 'lack of control' does not imply an attitude of indifference. On the contrary, one should see it as a genuine and profound commitment to difference, to change, to the dynamic. The references to science-fiction movies Ton Venhoeven regularly makes in formulating and explaining his architectural intentions do not emphasize the alien-ness of other civilizations. Rather, the scope seems to aim at the exposure of the alien-ness (or otherness) that lies within human culture. Alienating elements are always part of life, however strong the apparent need to dissolve or obliterate these elements. Humankind is fascinatingly creative in expressing 'other cultures' and wonderfully, yet intuitively, aware of the inherent estrangement of their own existence. Both our dependence on perception as the basis for 'reading' the world and the complex way our thinking is processing this perceptual information is causing a fragmented and discontinuous experience. One could refer to the biblical loss of paradise, or to Benjamin's interpretation of Paul Klee's Angel of History[46], if one wants to illustrate the attempt to understand the world as a whole and the inevitable failure to achieve this. Whether this 'coherent world' ever existed can probably never be determined. Not because the traces of its origins have disappeared, but because the original signs have been inscribed over and over again. From Libeskind's plea for Unoriginal Signs[47] to Derrida's statement 'there is nothing outside the text'[48], a tendency has by now become clear: contemporary society is constructed on 'linguistic games'[49]. Relating to a past that can no longer be remembered, only re-constructed, this practiced language results in the experience of drifting further into an abyss. This abyss is not a frightening void, nor an unavoidable End. Rather, this abyss has had its devastating attraction precisely because of its tentative mystery. Looking for things we do

46. Walter Benjamin, 'Theses on the Philosophy of History', in: Hannah Arendt (ed.), Illuminations (New York: 1969), pp. 257-258

47. Daniel Libeskind, Chamber Works; Architectural Meditations on Themes from Heraclitus, (London: Architectural Association, 1983)

48. Jacques Derrida, Of Grammatology (Baltimore: Johns Hopkins University Press, 1976)

49. Jean-François Lyotard, The Postmodern Condition; A Report on Knowledge (Minneapolis: University of Minnesota Press: 1984)

not understand, getting bored with any 'order of things' or any current state of knowledge that settles into fixed meanings and significances, the flight into the unknown seems to have become our r a i s o n - d ' ê t r e. Humanity's place in the universe is the starting framework for the search for understanding and meaning. At the same time it is clear that the borders of this framework remain unclear.

Like alien vessels, the objects in this story invade the city, creating a world of their own. Semi-detached from their surroundings, they stand as emblems of 'other' civilizations. The fact that these objects seem carefully embedded into their urban context (and, indeed, these contexts are always urban), only adds to the 'confusion'. A reason for this confusion could originate from the fact that VenhoevenCS' work increasingly aims at so-called 'strategies of denial'. These design strategies use techniques that evoke ambiguities and multiple readings. Whether these techniques refer to certain camouflage techniques, or to stealth technology or even to cloaking devices, is not so important in this context. The purpose is, in the end, to prevent a direct and clear reading of objects and spaces. Even though the objective of these strategies of denial is always heterogeneous, the result can be curiously homogeneous. Take the example of stealth technology, where the object is invisible to just one aspect of sensual experience or technical screening, while simultaneously being overly present in other related aspects. The F117-A Stealth fighter aircraft is famous for being invisible to radar and yet having a sound production that is extreme. The idea of inevitable multiple meanings surrounding an object can be formulated with more precision. In fact, the interrelatedness of the characteristics of an object make it too complex to allow one comprehensive reading. This would actually only be possible when the object itself is reproduced, including its specific external conditions.

VenhoevenCS' urban shapes seem to be folded into their definitive state. Anthony Vidler has interpreted the notion of the fold in precisely the same way. For him, the idea of the fold, as it had been introduced by Deleuze and Guatarri, represents 'constant movement' [50]. In the drawing Deleuze made of the Leibniz's folds, one can observe the schematic connection of the material sensing body on the ground with its 'monad' or soul on the

50. Antony Vidler (2000), p. 221

first floor. There is a certain restlessness inside the house that forms the basis of Vidler's interpretation of this diagram of the fold. The ambiguity of Deleuze's diagram is intriguing and confusing at the same time. Walter Benjamin used the same diagrammatic strategy reflecting the compulsive need to advance the meaning of an object from different angles. Benjamin's little diagram of the Arcades Project[51], connecting Paris with Naples, Moscow and Berlin, has been used to illustrate this method. It results in a condensed discourse that aims to achieve an endless debate of different readings.

Once the alien has landed in the urban context, an internal rupture occurs. The inner worlds are never as perfect as their outside shape suggests. The science fiction imagery is off-balance. The urban shapes are always complete and perfect, even when they represent a state of decay or destruction. Is this an architectural equivalent to the Trojan Horse? Is this an OASIS, an illusion evoked by a curious (mis)functioning of the senses? Once the skin has been transgressed, a world is revealed where any formal and spatial logic seems to have disappeared. The hectic and chaotic confrontations that occur in these inner worlds are caused by dazzling spatial interventions only. This is indeed a 'machine for living'; one that modifies experience and reflection through its staggering scenery in which one can move through a multiplicity of oblique planes, circulation elements, openings and cuts.

The material aspects of these buildings are straightforward. The architect does not mishandle form in relation to materials and details, and this is clearly a conscious statement. The tendency in contemporary architecture has been to over-emphasize the importance of applied materials in well-considered and detailed confrontations. In some of these projects, a building's unity cannot be disturbed by material collisions. In others, material collisions are made as if to represent the seeming instability of the structure. VenhoevenCS stays far away from these fashionable positions. Even his flirtations with the car industry – in the U2 project for instance – have a different function than the emphasis on the importance of the building's materiality. The critical relevance of architecture can never be

51. Susan Buck-Morss, The Dialectics of Seeing; Walter Benjamin and the Arcades Project (Cambridge/London: MIT Press, 1989), p. 25

only found in its materiality or its details. Rather, VenhoevenCS' material-ity is combining tactile experiences with representational readings.

This simultaneous 'presence' of the building thus achieves, even evokes, a transcendental experience that is crucial because it extends the unfold-ing of meanings. If aliens are 'only' the product of our imagination, so is the concept of the divine. If the urban forms play a game of denial, confus-ing the relation with the outer world, in the inner world one is forced into a forceful and direct confrontation. In these 'collisions', occurring in Ven-hoeven's inner worlds, one undergoes small 'accidents-waiting-to-happen'. Even if posed as an innocent side effect, presented with almost childish playfulness and aimed at provocation, the architectural work does intro-duce an uncanny, almost overwhelming, sense of fear and relief at the same time. This is, if one is willing to accept and thus 'see' it, indeed an architecture that is 'the site where technology may be cracked open by the imagination.' [52]

'To reiterate, a radical revision of architectural ideation and its true poten-tial (…) is urgently required. (…) These may be marginal and liminal places in our post-industrial culture, places where humanity may become aware of its capacity for true understanding in the dark and silent space of meta-phor, yet also the spaces within technology, revealing the actual presence of mortality, the immanence of Being.' [53]

52. Alberto Pérez-Gómez and Louise Pelletier, Architectural Representation and the Perspective Hinge (Cambridge/London: MIT Press, 1997), p. 395
53. Ibid.

56

THE WONDERFUL WORLD OF

OF ...

Network machines

In our current society, man has increasingly come to depend on networks for transfers and connections between people, places and objects. This growing mobility is giving rise to an increase in the space required for these networks. This may cause infrastructure to be transformed into a dangerous jungle, which has to be passed through on one's way home. [1]

(1)
MEDUSA'S HEAD
'Chris Burden's "Medusa's Head," a five-ton sphere of rock and concrete, does and does not live up to its name. As with the Medusa of myth, the sheer ugliness of Mr. Burden's new sculpture may stop some viewers in their tracks – and its startling levitation only adds to the effect. Measuring 14 feet in diameter, this scarred and craggy meteorlike mass hovers 2 feet above the floor in the otherwise empty main lobby of the Brooklyn Museum, its sole support a thick chain in the ceiling'. New York Times (12.07.1991), Section C, New York edition, p. 25, http://www.nytimes.com/1991/07/12/arts/review-art-medusa-s-head-without-the-snakes.html

59

In a metaphysical sense as well, these networks tend to occupy more and more space. The omnipresence of other places alongside one's own has a diverting effect in the here and now – similar to the way a mobile phone in a train compartment lets in the outside world into the capsule. A system then originates of parallel worlds that may overlap or cross one another. If such complicated places are situated close to each other in isolated territories, networks will change into interspaces that can be claimed from these different realities. Thus public space becomes a dealing space for different languages and cultures.

Several bodies and worlds can communicate by means of various networks and the techniques that come with them. By and large, such connecting infrastructural networks are looked upon purely as instrumental elements, as tools allowing our bodies to move speedily. This purely utilitarian outlook is, however, unsatisfactory: networks and technologies also lead their own lives, with the attendant risks and opportunities.

We are becoming more and more conscious of the way we have become part of all kinds of global networks, because ever more connections are being spread all over the world. They may well come in handy, those networks, but they are also going to shape a new reality. We have come to live in a shrinking world where formerly independent cultures have to learn to live with 'others' next door. Originally the networks were developed as useful utilities, as a sort of extensions of our body in the sense that they enlarge the area where we can act and one can still experience the advantages of that original idea: without actually going there, in the Netherlands we can reach for products and ideas in China and vice versa, simply by pressing the buttons of our computer.[2] But the networks needed to achieve this, increasingly encroach upon our lives. Not only we can grab something from far away, others can also grab things from the formerly safe places where we live ourselves. New forms of communications make us mobile and we can be reached anywhere.[3] At any time of the day our mobile phone may ring or we may receive an e-mail. Nowadays, the 'other' is omnipresent in our environment. You can drive anywhere comfortably by car, but on a road that in itself also causes inconvenience or discomfort for others.[4] We tend to ignore this by retiring more and more into our specially designed, comforting capsules. Mobile, static and virtual and mental capsules are everywhere, designed and considered to be safe havens.[5] From there we look at the world as a dangerous place to live in, paradoxically becoming more and more frightened of 'others' we do not know. Learning to enjoy the discomfort of networks and the encounters with these 'others' that networks bring to our lives and learning to appreciate them as inevitable and valuable part of our environment, learning to enjoy that whole new environment as the new n a t u r e, instead of only using the utilitarian networks for their purposes, is one of the big challenges for contemporary culture. In this, we can learn a lot from scenario writers and moviemakers because at least from Charlie Chaplin's M o d e r n   T i m e s, they try to develop new ways to appreciate life in the networks. Jim Jarmusch in S t r a n g e r   T h a n   P a r a d i s e and Coppola in L o s t   i n   T r a n s l a - t i o n, use the adventures and pitfalls of life in the network society as their favourite subjects.[6]

62

(2)
SUBURBS AND CARBON FUELS
A different example is the creation of suburbs. They became popular as an opportunity to seek an alternative to crowded metropolis.

Development of suburbs was enabled by innovations in transportation as well as public subsidies that bore the cost of infrastructure such as roads, water and electricity. The trend toward decentrated urban form was further advanced by the advent of the automobile culture and the availability of unprecedented amounts of energy in the form of carbon fuels.

See also: w w w . w i k i p e d i a . o r g

(3)
AIBO
To fight loneliness in our comfortable but lonely capsules, Sony invented the AIBO. 'The fascinating AIBO concept is part of the very conscious ambition from Sony to create intelligent companions for people. To achieve this, a groundbreaking vision to combine Sony flagship technologies with Artificial Intelligence was pursued. The result: a unique companion, gradually adapting itself to your environment, capable of

expressing emotion, very skilful, and with an inherent desire to entertain.' – S o n y   A I B O   E R S - 7   (M I N D 3) brochure – 2005/2006 edition

(4)
THE CITY AND THE CAR
'Former President of France, Pompidou, said "il faut adapter Paris à l'automobile". Paris became an object, which had to be adapted to another object. This is the world of Cyborg. You have to adapt to that world. You are living in that world and your life is completely determined by it.' – Augustin Berque, 'On the Chinese Origins of Cyborgs Hermitage in the Absolute Market', in: T h e   G l o b a l   C i t y   a n d   t h e   T e r r i t o r y; history, theory, critique (Eindhoven: 2001) p. 31

(5)
CAPSULE/CYBORG
'The capsule is cyborg architecture. Man, machine and space build a new organic body, which transcends confrontation. (...) it creates an environment in itself. (...) A device, which has become a living space in itself in the sense that man cannot hope to live elsewhere, is a

capsule. And signs of such developments are beginning to appear around us.' – Kisho Kurokawa, 1969

(6)
THE NETWORK AND THE CAPSULE
'Due to the use of ships, cars, aircraft, television and the Internet, the global network economy has tightened its grip upon our lives. These days the form and nature of our living environment are determined by the influence of global networks rather than by social, geographic and spatial properties of our direct environment. This is why we are discussing the rise of network societies and the network city. The network city is made possible because capsules – such as ships, cars, trains and aircraft. With the help of screens and digital networks of television and computer we can make virtual choices how we move about in this world. In this way we can decide what should be part of our environment, which people and things we are prepared to admit to our social world and which to refuse entry. (...) a large number of theoreticians has published critical texts on the network society. Books with titles

like A m e r i c a (Jean Baudrillard), N e g a t i v e   H o r i z o n (Paul Virilio), E c o l o g y   o f   F e a r (Mike Davis), T h e   F a l l   o f   P u b l i c   M a n (Richard Sennett), D e   A n g s t m a c h i n e (T h e   F e a r   M a c h i n e, René Boomkens), S p h e r e s (S p h ä r e n   I and S p h ä r e n   I I , Peter Sloterdijk) and T h e   C a p s u l a r   C i v i l i z a t i o n, (Lieven De Cauter), deal with various problems of the network society. They draw attention to the emergence of g a t e d   c o m m u n i t i e s in the United States and to comparable phenomena in other countries.

In the Netherlands too these g a t e d   c o m m u n i t i e s are emergent. More and more developers of housing projects are focusing on specific target groups and are tailoring the language of urban development and architectural design accordingly. One can readily conclude that the resulting flight of the white middle class from mixed cities has intensified segregation enormously. In all kinds of places a certain degree of ghettoization is taking place and this is a clear sign of capsularization.' – Ton Venhoeven, Inaugural speech, 3 November 2006, University of Technology Eindhoven

Eilanders kunnen niet wachten

Jan Schaefer Bridge
and Warehouse De Zwijger
Amsterdam, 2001

moet nog officieel worden geopend, maar de bewoners van het Java-eiland kunnen daar niet op wachten. Hoewel hekken de toegan neter lange brug belemmeren en er nog veel bouwafval ligt, gebruiken dagelijks, en vooral aan het begin van de avond, tallo 's deze brug, die het eiland verbindt met de stad.
FOTO JOHANNES ABEL

So when I was working on the design of the bridge to Java Island in Amsterdam, I did not take the idea of a heroic connection as a starting point, but instead, focussed on the network's own life. I just could not get the thought out of my mind how I could kiss such a bridge to life so that the thing would lead its own life. What I wanted to show and dramatize was the monumental event of a network attacking an existing warehouse and the everyday event of people and vehicles crossing this bridge. To incorporate this animistic idea, you have to be able to integrate different perspectives of people and objects into one single design. To simultaneously make a functionally perfect and economically feasible bridge, we always work in teams, like filmmakers with lots of different specialists. That is one of the things that CS in VenhoevenCS stands for.

63

Haarlems Dagblad
6-1-2001

Salamander groeit in Amsterdam

AMSTERDAM • De Jan Schaefferbrug, ook wel bekend als De Salamander, krijgt gestalte in Amsterdam. De brug, die uit vijf delen bestaat, ligt middels gedeeltelijk op zijn plek. Als hij is voltooid, ontstaat er een verbinding voor fietsers en wandelaars tussen het Java-eiland en de Oostelijke Handelskade aan het IJ. Op de Oostelijke Handelskade gaat de brug dwars door een oud pakhuis.
FOTO • ANP • ROBBERT SLAGMAN

Drie bruggen!

Wintermans: de brug als vlieggend object.

De gemeenteraad heeft pas begin dit jaar besloten dat de Javabrug verhoogd door het pakhuis de Zwijger boven een enigszins verlaagde Veemkade zal gaan lopen. De planvorming is daardoor vertraagd, maar binnenkort liggen er dan toch drie ontwerpen voor de Javabrug ter inzage. De ontwerpen zijn het resultaat van een prijsvraag onder drie architecten. Dit zijn Ton Venhoeven, Paul Wintermans van architectenbureau Quist-Wintermans, en de architecten Verburg en Hoogendijk. Elk ontwerp heeft zijn eigen beeld en elk van de bruggen heeft een andere specifieke constructie.

— MAARTEN DANKERS

In het reglement van de prijsvraag stonden de randvoorwaarden waaraan de brug moest voldoen. Zo werden er eisen gesteld aan de hellingshoek, aan de vrije doorvaarthoogte en natuurlijk aan het maximaal te besteden budget. Bijzonder

brug zélf. Als je de brug zou aanleggen als een platte 'plank', dan zou hij doorzakken. Er moet dus iets bedacht worden om dit te voorkomen. Bij het doorbuigen ontstaan er allerlei drukken trekkrachten in de constructie, die moeten worden opgevangen. Dit kan

Jan Schaefer Bridge – a sneaky reptile

In 1995 we received the order to make a study into the possibilities of building a bridge right through an existing warehouse and ending on the head of Java Island in Amsterdam. It was a very interesting assignment for us because of the linking up of objects that are normally like cat and dog.

65

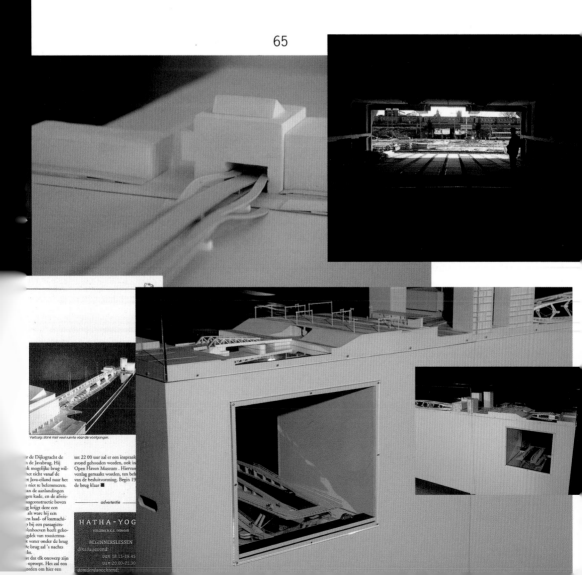

Voetweg: stank niet veel ruimte voor de voetganger.

r de Dijksgracht de
n de Javabrug. Hij
k mogelijke brug wil-
et richt vanaf de
t Java-eiland naar het
nier te belemmeren.
an de aanlandingen
gen kade, en de afwis-
agonstructie boven
g krijgt deze een
als ware hij een
en laad- of losmachi-
bij een passagiers-
nboven heeft geko-
gdek van roosterma-
water onder de brug
e brug zal 's nachts
ht.
t dat elk ontwerp zijn
oproept. Het zal een
orden om hier een

tot 22 00 uur zal er een inspraak
avond gehouden worden, ook in
Open Haven Museum . Hiervan
verslag gemaakt worden, ten beh
van de besluitvorming. Begin 19
de brug klaar ■

AMSTERDAM – Werknemers van bouwcombinatie Ballast Nedam - Hollandia plaatsten gisteren het sluitstuk van de Jan Schaeferbrug. De brug, die het Jav... Handelskade verbindt is een ontwerp van architect Ton Venhoeve. De 280 meter lange brug loopt dwars door het pakhuis 'De Zwijger'. (Foto NRC Handels...

The assignment of making a bridge collide with a building, was the result of a planning accident. It had been decided that a bridge had to be built to the Island. But at the other end, on the quay, there was a former warehouse, which a pressure group wanted to preserve as an example of architectural heritage. We gave form to this starting point in the most direct way: we proposed to make a wound in the building; a hole in the warehouse that would make its bowels visible. To create a crossing of the quay on different levels, this big hole had to be drilled right through the heart of the warehouse.

66

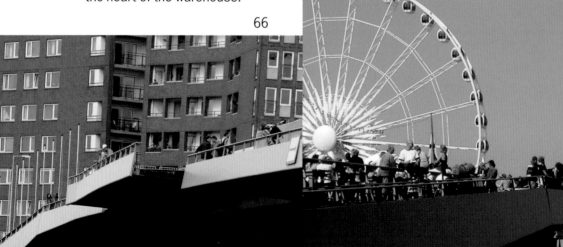

Next to that, two parts of the bridge had to be removable. Every five years these parts are taken out with a view to the SAIL Amsterdam event. On this kind of occasion the bridge could also become a sort of stand, a theatre from which you would be able to watch the age-old vessels using the water infrastructure. On top of that, a group of people announced that they were interested in using the building as a cultural centre for new media. All this could make the building, the bridge and the people using them into a vibrant, theatrical public place. Here, the various forms of physical and virtual infrastructure could make people and objects meet, with everyday experiences, connections and cultural events as a result.[7]

67

(7)
(NO) MORE ILLUSION

The design reacted strongly to what I experienced shortly before in Los Angeles as 'a preview of the gated society to come': 'The community hype of recent years has been tending more and more to produce xenophobic mini-utopias in which early twentieth century ideals of outdoor living, the good country life, the American dream and the more recent 'recreation oriented lifestyle' have become interwoven with concepts of the neighbourhood watch and armed response. The notorious dullness of such suburbs is counterbalanced by the fastest growing branch of the world economy: entertainment. While the anxiety and dread of violence increase day by day, fed by intensive media coverage of anything that can possibly reinforce prejudices about safety and danger, the market for horror movies takes on gigantic proportions. Music, video, Disney and Las Vegas are the chief substitute experiences for safe living and safe sex. At the same time, travel to far-off, exotic places is heavily promoted by the tourism industry.'

Venhoeven, Ton, '(No) more illusion: safety in LA', Archis, nr. 1 (1995), p. 69

Then the bridge itself, for that is what it was all about. For bridges, mostly an arch or suspended structure is utilized, which often results in a gate-like effect. But in this case the gate was there already, really, in the shape of the warehouse that we had to drill through. We did not want to add another triumphal arch. We preferred the breakthrough to be the gate. In the mean time we had to bear in mind that apart from the main route, which was approaching on a different level, there had to be cycle paths and pedestrian bridges as well that were supposed to connect to the two quays.

73

lesprogramma op de Jan Schaeferbrug, april 2002 foto's: bureau ARCAM

t ontwerp van René
ij de opzet van deze
ende rol gespeeld.

AM NUTSHELL is
in 2002. Doel van
storisch schema,
terdamse architec-
orische context
akt aan bij diverse
van 2003 zullen
svinden en waar-
s achtergrond kan
nde evenementen

Almost as a rule, humans tend to deal with infrastructure rather thoughtlessly. We keep on talking about the function and never about the road itself. Asphalt and bridges are instrumental in bearing cars and will never protest. Therefore, in this specific case, we decided to focus on the bridge proper, to show and shape it as a concentration of infrastructure and give it the form of a living thing, even an animal, perhaps. The infrastructure, represented by the various networks had to get a face and become visible, rather than its intended purpose, the seamless connection between two quays. The idea was to turn asphalt into a living subject.

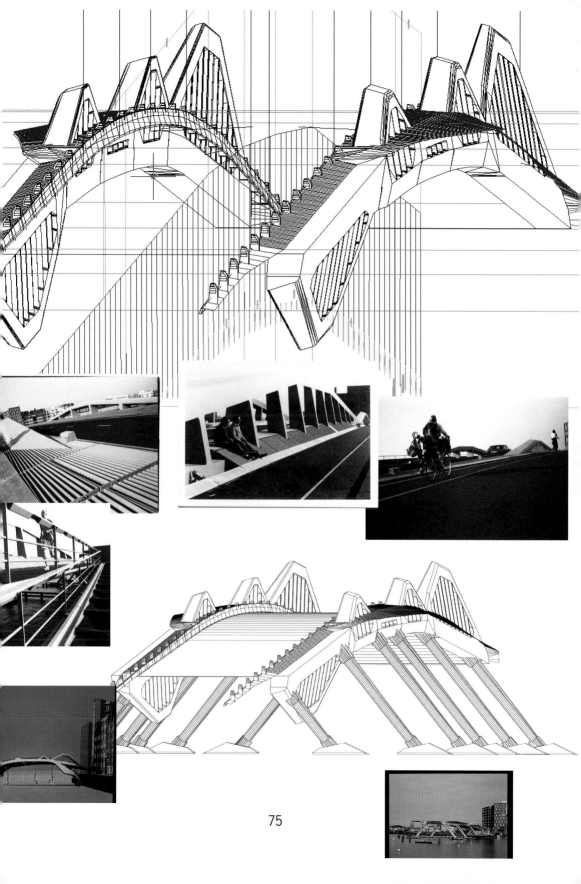

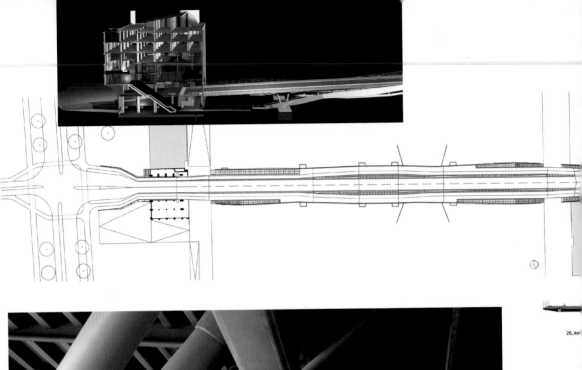

26,4m

34,8m

43,2m

51,6m

60,0m

68,4m

Because we really had to compress the bridge where it penetrates the building, we had to move certain parts of the construction to a position under the bicycle lanes. What you get with the converging and divergent lines in the construction of the bridge, the bicycle lanes, the stairs and footpaths, are accelerated and decelerated perspectives. We thought it was fascinating to try and use this to make every metre of this animistic bridge appear differently. In this way the perception constantly passes through changes of interpretation, depending on where you walk, ride a bicycle or drive a car. This bridge turns a daily crossing into an everyday event and interactive cinematic experience.

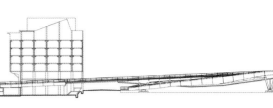

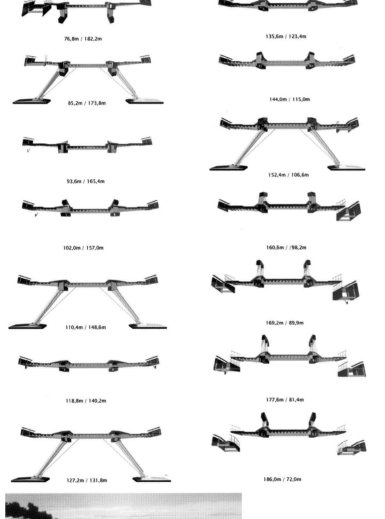

76,8m / 182,2m

135,6m / 123,4m

202,8m / 56,2m

85,2m / 173,8m

144,0m / 115,0m

211,2 m / 47,8m

93,6m / 165,4m

152,4m / 106,6m

219,6m / 39,4m

102,0m / 157,0m

160,6m / /98,2m

228,0m / 31,0m

110,4m / 148,6m

169,2m / 89,9m

236,4m / 22,6m

118,8m / 140,2m

177,6m / 81,4m

244,8m / 14,2m

127,2m / 131,8m

186,0m / 72,0m

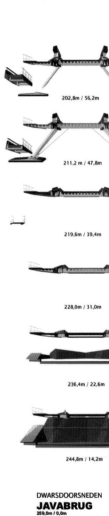

DWARSDOORSNEDEN
JAVABRUG
259,0m / 0,0m

Houthavens – tunnel with bridges and square

Networks for traffic take up a lot of space and can divide neighbourhoods. When the city of Amsterdam wanted to make a new harbour front development, the existing artery along the river IJ caused major problems. Pedestrian networks were blocked and traffic noise made it very difficult to comply with noise regulations.

81

Tunnel boulevard Houthavens
Amsterdam, 2003

Pedestrians are at other moments car drivers, so we grabbed the opportunity to improve the routings for both. Pedestrians experience a slight acclivity before descending to the newly constructed islands, drivers experience a strange perspective as they see the world from just above the water surface. At some places, eyes can meet.

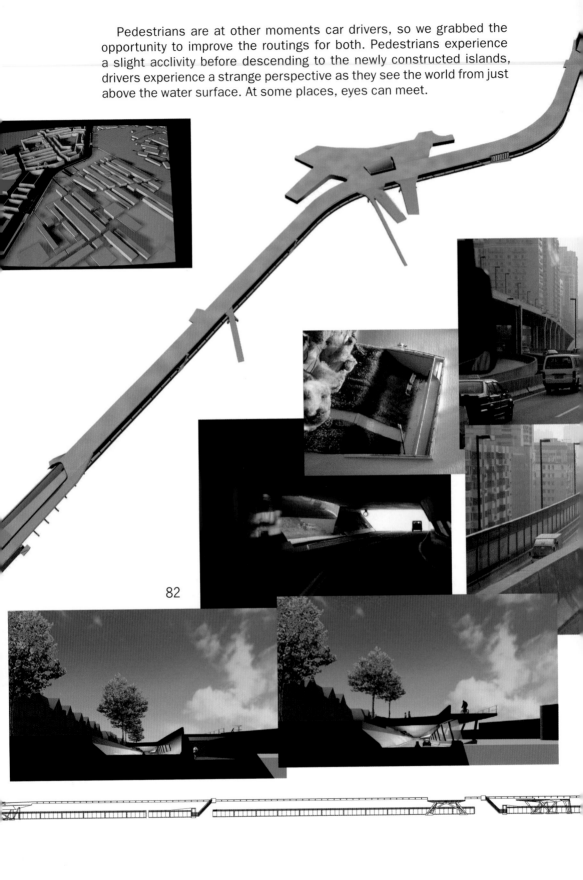

84

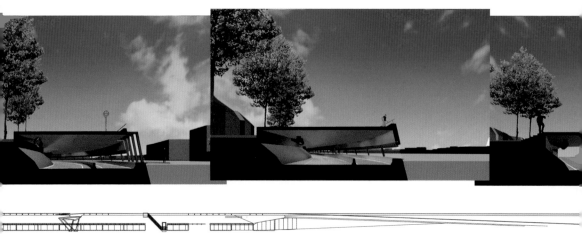

In an innovative combination of tunnel, public boulevard, square and pedestrian bridges, the square and bridges are situated between the existing neighbourhood and the new. Instead of stacking prototypical elements on top of each other, a continuous skin is stretched and wrapped over all the different parts. With this, the design explores the different definitions of these elements: the tunnel can also be read as a mole, an animal digging just below the surface, or as a hollow and transparent dike, the bridges can be read as square with holes or as jetties to the banks of the new islands, the square can be read as a series of bridges, a traffic node, a pedestrian roundabout or a square with a number of holes, the whole architectural element can be seen as a snail or some unknown, composed strange animal, or a tunnel in disguise. With this ambiguity, the real character of this new infrastructural element is suspended, creating numerous using opportunities. An important issue if you want infrastructure to survive as long as possible.

85

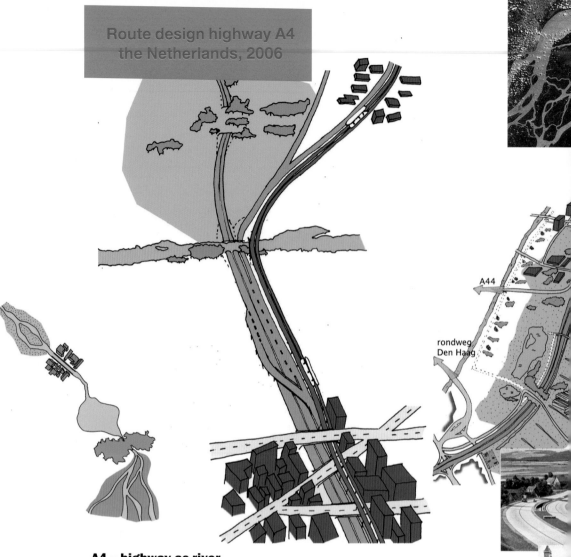

A44

rondweg
Den Haag

A4 – highway as river

Many highways were originally designed as Arcadian parkways, or sublime passages through overwhelming, unspoilt mountain ranges. To be consequent in pleasing the driver's experience, even passages through cities where adorned with parks and trees, as for example Moses' highway designs for New York show. It lasted until the late fifties before designers saw the opportunity to create sublime passages with flyovers through high-rise urban landscapes. We can still find beautiful remnants of that time in many Asian cities, but in Europe flyovers are rapidly torn down. There, many urban highways are partially or completely put in tunnels. Outside the downtown areas, suburbs with sound screens and barriers have grown along the arteries, blocking motorist's views and pedestrian and animal's transversal connections. Further on, the former parkways and sublime mountain passages are disappearing behind scattered buildings and advertisings. This development turned driving on highways and living around it into pretty depressing experiences. Car infrastructure tends to cause trouble and unexpected building activities everywhere.

For this reason, the Dutch government started a programme to improve the spatial quality and public image of highway infrastructure. We were asked to design a spatial strategy for highway A4, which connects Amsterdam to The Hague, Rotterdam and Antwerp. The A4 is a partly existing and partly projected highway through the delta of the rivers Rhine and Meuse. In the northern part it cuts through main ports like Schiphol Airport and the harbour of Rotterdam and many suburbs, in the southern part it (still) runs or will run through agricultural lands, before it hits Antwerp across the border with Belgium.

Our plan aims at transforming the highway over a long period of time: something like fifty years. To transform the A4 into a beautiful, sustainable highway, many measures have to be taken. To reduce energy consumption and inefficient land use and to make multimodal connections possible, new buildings must be built in existing urban areas. Worn-out ugly buildings in the middle of nowhere should be demolished and new buildings in the landscape should be prohibited. Second, multimodal traffic networks with a complementary combination of car infrastructure, public transport, bicycle lanes and pedestrian walkways have to be developed and short-circuited. Cities have to become attractive for families and singles, factories and businesses, plants and animals, mixed as far as possible. This way, traffic flow on the highway can be restored and energy use by traffic be diminished. Cars have to become clean and silent. Energy for traffic should be harvested from the sun. Transversal relations – both in the cities and in rural areas – for animals and people have to be restored. Asphalt can be used to collect energy from the sun and from passing traffic. Roadsides should become healthy biotopes. In the long run, the environment of the highway can become a healthy and attractive place to live, like the quays of a river downtown.

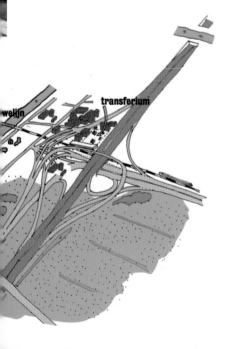

**Heijplaat Playground
Rotterdam, 1994**

Heijplaat – the world as playground

The rise of global networks causes minor and major tragedies everywhere. As a consequence of new legislation curbing environmental pollution near residential areas, the village of Heijplaat ran into difficulties.
The village is situated in the middle of the Rotterdam dock area, a major
transport hub and driving force behind this country's economy. According to the standards set by new legislation, the village could no longer
exist in the middle of the harbour, so the village almost became a victim
of growing global networks. And it really was a popular place to live. The
intended demolition caused strong opposition on the part of the local
residents, who had lived here for generations and who's children loved
playing in run down parts of the harbour area. After a lot of campaign-
ing and struggles with politics, an exception to the law was devised for
three specific cities, one of which was Heijplaat. To make amends, the
Rotterdam Harbour Board donated a playground and VenhoevenCS was
asked to design it in a workshop with a group of international students.

90

Children use their fantasy a lot, so all over the world children love playing at places or with objects that are not designed as specific playgrounds or overdesigned toys. In general this is a good preparation for life in societies that are also not only tailored for their comfort. We used this assignment to make an adventure playground out of second hand harbour materials, a miniature world with a village of containers, mountains of collapsed bridges and rejected piles, tunnels of sewers, a jungle in a climbing cage of wire mesh, trenches or a graveyard – depending on a child's fantasy – of platform elements, a wasteland with possibilities to build your own hut and a theatre podium in an open container. We reused some elements like a climbing aeroplane – we turned it into a crashed aeroplane in the jungle – and a classical evergreen: the merry-go-round. All this was wrapped around a desert (that could be used as a soccer field too).

Every object has multiple playing possibilities: a pile as part of a mountain range can become a bus or a bench to watch the theatre, depending on the situation, a sewer can become a story of a chase or an adventurous passage to the world of the aliens, just as a collapsed bridge can become an adventurous passage through the Himalayas. Because this is not a place where things are designed to make one feel comfortable, it is the perfect Alice in Wonderland for children to learn to deal with the life of things and the unexpected events that come with it.

This whole world was folded around an even more miniature world defended by dwarfs and fences. Here the youngest children can play safely to exercise their skills before they will be allowed to play in the adventure world.[8]

(8)
PLAYGROUNDS
Our childhood memories reveal that scarcely any of us has ever played in a playground. What we do remember are play areas that were never intended as such: waste lands, dug up roads, shrubs and bushes, fields, a bizarre tree, an attic or cellar, a building site, the stairwell, a place under a table. One person's memories kindle those of others and before long there is a mountain of material. Now and then we talk with hands and feet. At-mosphere, noises and smells are not easy to capture in words. Everybody has his own world of memories and realities.'
Venhoeven, Ton, 'Heyplaat', in: Jan de Graaf, Gijs Wallis de Vries (eds), Riverine Architecture: an anthology of workship Holland (Rotterdam: 010 Publishers, 1994), p. 81

Laboratory of the Food
and Consumer Product Safety Authority
Zwijndrecht, 2003

Laboratory – a controlling network

How can one visualize the autonomy of things that are only meant to have a function for humans? Is it possible to give a controlling network mechanism a real face?[9] This theme occupies central stage in many B-movies, but it also exercises the minds at our office. It was a matter of course that in the Palace of Versailles the staff remained invisible and that was also true for the British <u>upstairs-downstairs</u> culture. Meanwhile we have become used to the fact that servants, people who provide services, have become visible. This is part of their social emancipation. The strange thing is, however, that the material and the organic do not take part in this emancipation. All kinds of things that lend a helping hand in social processes remain virtually unnoticed.

(9)
CAPSULAR SOCIETY

'A society of mobility is unthinkable without omnipresent control. Whereas the disciplinary society was based on interiorization, the control society functions externally: through militarization of the urban space. The technological devices, however, with their soft, almost invisible thresholds, do not suffice. The simultaneously archaic and hypermodern 'primal fact' of architecture and urbanism of the twenty-first century will be: the fence, the wall, the gate, the stronghold. Because a separation of worlds never works, and the populations of the second, third and fourth world are spreading out and are by now everywhere, the first world is no longer a homogeneous empire with relatively homogeneous territory, but an archipelago of fortresses and strongholds. Transport becomes to an increasing degree the transit between controlled and closed-off zones. The generic city is obsessed by closing-off, safety and control. One can appropriately term this "the cellular city", and even the "capsular civilization".' – Lieven De Cauter, autumn 1998

96

Breeding pack animals seems a natural thing to do, just like building the machines that derived from them and all the other objects and things that we use to make our lives safe and comfortable. We take their servitude for granted. At the same time, when overdone, comfort and safety may lead to a capsular life and fear of others, causing social and medical disorders as a result.[10]

Many instruments have unpredictable consequences. Although their behaviour may seem to be controllable under laboratory circumstances, most of them not only achieve what they are designed for, but have other cultural and biological effects as well. In a complex everyday environment, many instruments behave uncontrollably, as if they have a life of their own. Just look at an instrument like language![11] We expect the words to serve our purposes, but many times, because they can be interpreted in many different ways, they are understood slightly or totally different, as if the words have a will of their own. Therefore, the architecture of the laboratory of the Food & Consumer Product Safety Authority had this animistic idea of emancipating the world of the objects as a point of departure. We could have designed an inconspicuous and efficient building, but we felt that it would be more appropriate to visualize the organization's processes and their multiple meanings through an advanced form of 'architecture parlante'. Giving a face to the organization's underlying ideology has been made into the main motive of the design.

(10)
SPHERES

'The multifarious subcultures of the modern social systems – whether they are organizations or private spheres – form variegated fleets of arks of different sizes, which navigate the unremitting flood of environmental complexity in an entirely individual way. But nowadays no one releases doves carrying olive branches to bring the message that all is well in his own world. Postmodernity has abandoned the dream of a safe landing after the flood. What was once flood is now land. If all that is left are absolute houses, each with its own course, a return to what was once called land has become impossible.'- Sloterdijk Peter, Sferen (Spheres) (Amsterdam: Uitgeverij Boom, 2003)

p. 580 Translation from Sphären I and Sphären II (Frankfurt am Main: Suhrkamp, 1998/1999)

(11)
CYBORG

Comfort and fear producing capsules are not only physical machines and they are not detached from the human body either. When you consider that even language is a utensil, it is hard to think of yourself outside of all the utensils that surround you; our bodies and capsules are united beings and inhabit a world of Cyborgs. The logic of language is a difficult companion to achieve cultural change.

'Back to the problem of Cyborg. We know Cyborg as a being that is half organic and half mechanical, cybernetic. But this is only the image we know

from the movies. We think we are not Cyborg, except for some people who need some mechanical parts in their body to survive. This is a very limited conception of a Cyborg. The techniques extend our functions. But what do the symbols do? They retrieve the world within our body. When I speak of the planet Mars here, Mars is not here physically, but it goes through my body, because the symbol enables me to represent it and it goes outside of my mouth to your ears into your bodies. So the symbols brought Mars back here. This is a movement of going in and going out. It is both a "cosmization" and a "somatization". So your body becomes a world and "somatization" means your world becomes your body. If our world is dominated by a logic of objective systems,

a system of objects in a modern way, it becomes a mechanical world. This mechanical world is retrieved into our own body and by doing this, it imposes this mechanical logic to our own existence.' -

Augustin Berque, 'On the Chinese Origins of Cyborg's Hermitage in the Absolute Market,' in: The Global City and the Territory, Proceedings of the International Architecture Conference, TU/e (Eindhoven: TU/e, 2001) p.31

97

The cultural concept of the lab and the network that it is part of is to improve society by means of improving the quality and reliability of products. The building functions as the eyes and ears of the central government. In our society, improving safety sounds as a good target, but many specialists argue that supposedly 'safe' products can also create a false idea of safety. In safe cars, accidents are caused because you do not feel speed and when your body is not used to dealing with dangerous bacteria, you fall ill the first day you are in a contaminated environment. Also, children that play with dull but safety tested playground equipment always find ways to use it in a more adventurous way. Total and absolute safety is not something that can be achieved.

To put it boldly, the purpose of this lab design is to stimulate safety and hygiene and not to take safety and hygiene too seriously. So we have visualized the building, the road, the cars and the surrounding events to the same extent as the interior organization of the building, as a connected network machine and terminal. In this composition each part is in cooperation with all other parts.

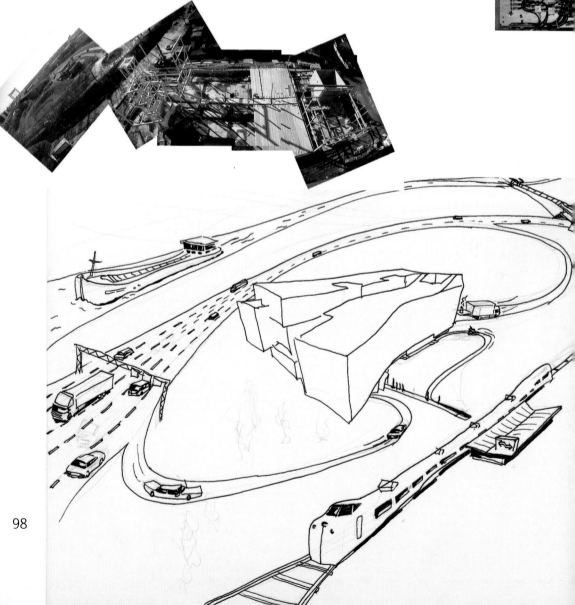

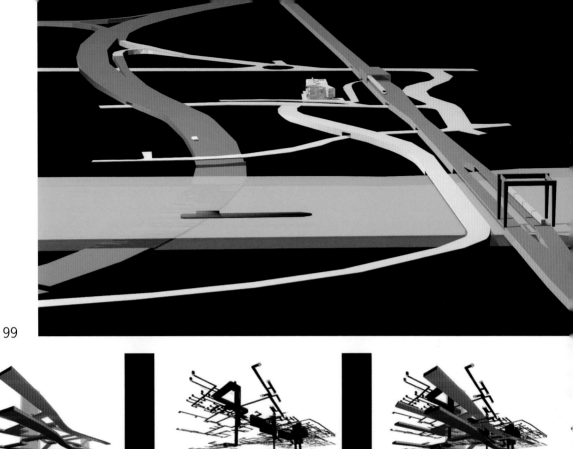

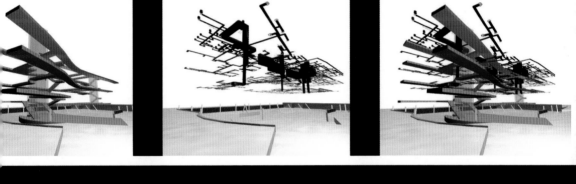

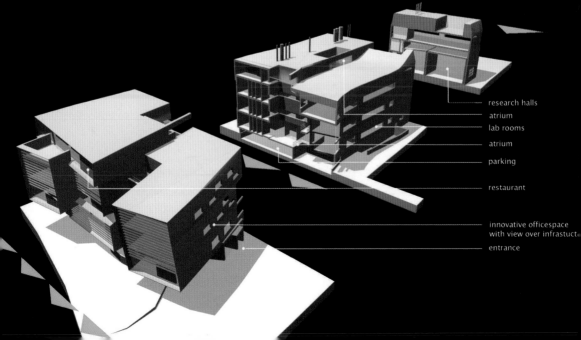

research halls
atrium
lab rooms
atrium
parking

restaurant

innovative officespace
with view over infrastuct

entrance

But this alone does not turn a network node into a living object. For that purpose we conceived the interior as a separate world in which every space is the most important in its own way. The new building had to accommodate three departments and each demanded a different form of space with a view to its use. Offices had to be bright, flexible, neutral and full of character, and offer a good working environment for the varying project teams. The laboratories asked for a simple rectangular plan with as little influence from outside as possible. Likewise the examination halls for coarse tests on large objects demanded very specific dimensions and acoustic qualities. True, all places – test hall, car park, office – can derive justification and character from the functional position within the organization of the building, but outside of that logic, one can also look at the different spaces as separate and connected living environments, independent of their function to serve something else. When moving from one place to another in this building, one can see how the interpretation of the whole is changing all the time. To keep all these different spaces together, the skin of the building has been stretched around this complex body.

To connect the different spaces spatially, we made visibility lines in the building connecting the offices with the laboratories and the workshops at the other end. Also, we transformed the age-old idea of atrium and impluvium where light penetrating a building from above would create heavenly axes with small fountains reflecting the sky above. Also in our project life revolves around these mythic centres but here it is not just humans living around them. Many parts of the building witness the light from above as well.

101

Assuming that organizations and the world of objects have lives and purposes of their own implicates that the organization's or building's influence on the future of the world is unpredictable. Thus not building instruments, but creating unpredictable events is the essence that drives the development of culture. Also, the design and building process become as important an event as the intended result of the function of the building. Building and designing as 'event', can become top-class sport if everybody is determined to get the most out of it. In 'making', the state of technology and its possibilities is crucial to the end result.

For this building a construction was needed that did justice to the flow of the processes and the diverse nature of the various inner spaces. The skin should be flexible and at the same time be able to represent the modernity, hybridity and fluidity of the network organization and the interior of the building as a social environment. During the design process other specialists explained to us how complex constructions could be utilized to achieve this and how a tailor-made aluminium skin with multiple folds could be made to measure in the factory. With these techniques we could make a very flexible structure and skin.

People using different networks during their lives develop different perspectives on reality and react accordingly different to events that occur around them. This not a bad thing but a blessing. 'Misunderstanding' is relative, the production of all kinds of different interpretations fuels the production of ideas and languages that propel the course of events in the world. That is why I am very interested in the way that signs can refer to different realities at the same time. By simultaneous reference to different worlds, a building can become a cultural icon instead of a disciplining device, the building becomes a connection or a junction in the various ways people experience their version of reality.

103

This idea can be traced in many of our projects. I do not mean to say that this building for example refers to thousands of things, but definitely to six or seven at the same time and in a way that is incomplete per reference. On top of that, because of this incompleteness every individual is invited to develop different connotations. It does not matter when users or spectators fail to grasp certain meanings; there is always a key for some form of understanding.

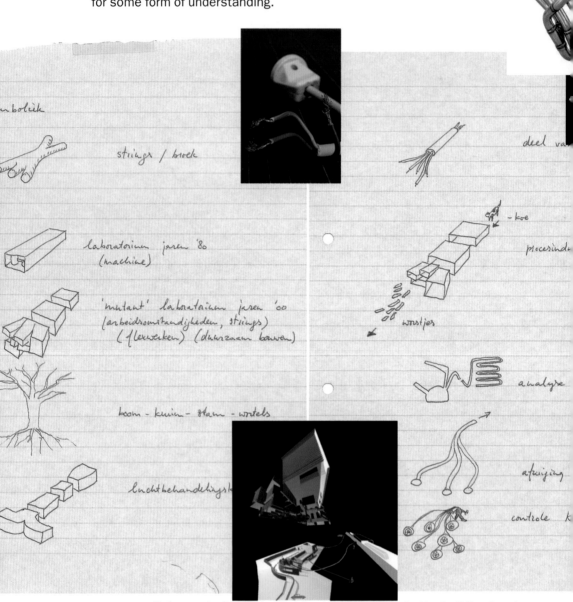

Being part of a controlling hygienistic network, the building has been designed like a terminal. Half of the employees are not in the building, but on their way somewhere in the car or at a location that needs examining. The information collected by the inspectors is of an extremely miscellaneous nature. One brings samples into the lab, the other digital info and a third person chemical material or a piece of playground equipment. For all this input the building is a machine, processing objects, food and information. The results of the tests and analyses are channelled to the Ministry, that uses them to take legal measures.

Then there is the meaning of the apparatus and the context of apparatuses in the surroundings. The laboratory in Zwijndrecht is situated among former shipyards along the river Merwede. There used to be a great many vast shipyards in the various Drecht towns, big sheds serving as terminals for ship repair. Hence the reference to a repair shed, even though this one is a s p a c e-version of it. The building is a kind of terminal in the physical context and a mother spaceship in the children's fantasy world of films and games.

In an entirely different field, viz. that of theoretical physics, the building refers to the cosmological string theory. The laboratory is a research machine aimed at analyzing reality. When you reduce the idea of research to its most fundamental basis, you end up in the search for the essence of things: the unifying string theory. We have attempted to visualize the idea of strings in the building – similar to how in the old days the cosmic timepiece served as inspiration for architects designing machine-like buildings.[12] Moreover I think strings are also interesting from a linguistic point of view: the theory abandons the idea that the micro world consists of a collection of loose particles for a grand unifying idea: we name them as different particles, but in fact they could be mere oscillations of energy. Each different kind of oscillation is seen and interpreted as different particle. How we name particles, depends on how we interpret different oscillations.[13]

(12)
COSMIC TIMEPIECE
In this sense, modern science is a continuation of the ageless efforts of man to organize and exploit the world in which he lives. (...) We still use, or have used until quite recently, Neolithic techniques (...) Our social organization was for a long time based on the same techniques of writing, geometry, and arithmetic as those required to organize the hierarchically differentiated and structured social groups of the Neolithic city states. Thus we cannot help acknowledging the continuity that exists between Neolithic techniques and the scientific and industrial revolutions.' (Prigogine Ilya, Stengers Isabelle, Order out of Chaos (Toronto, New York, London, Sydney) p. 37)
Why did the clock almost immediately become the very symbol of world order? In this last question lies perhaps some elements of an answer. A watch is a contrivance governed by a rationality that lies outside itself, by a plan that is blindly executed by its inner workings. The clock world is a metaphor suggestive of God the Watchmaker, the rational master of a robotlike nature. At the origine of modern science, a resonance appears to have been set up between theological discourse and theoretical and experimental activity – a "resonance" that was no doubt likely to amplify and consolidate the claim that scientists were in the progress of discovering the secret of the 'great machine of the universe'. Ibid. p. 46

(13)
STRING THEORY
'In the last few decades, string theory has emerged as the most promising candidate for a microscopic theory of gravity. And it is infinitely more ambitious than that: it attempts to provide a complete, unified, and consistent description of the fundamental structure of our universe. The essential idea behind string theory is this: all of the different 'fundamental' particles of the Standard Model are really just different manifestations of one basic object: a string. How can that be? Well, we would ordinarily picture an electron, for instance, as a point with no internal structure. A point cannot do anything but move. But, if the string theory is correct, then under an extremely powerful 'microscope' we would realize that the electron is not really a point, but a tiny loop of string. A string can do something aside from moving – it can oscillate in different ways. If it oscillates a certain way, then from a distance, unable to tell it is really a string, we see an electron. But if it oscillates some other way, well, then we call it a photon, or a quark, or a (...) you get the idea. So, if string theory is correct, the entire world is made of strings.' — Alberto Güijosa, www.nuclecu. unam.mx/~alberto/phys- ics/string.html

The reference to the String theory may be something one can only see when reflecting on the building, so for the people working within the building it may have an entirely different meaning. The different laboratories that had to be integrated in this regional headquarter wanted to see their own, mutually different and sometimes even competing working methods and rituals translated in the functional layout of the building. People who want to see it that way can say that the building is the perfect body to solve the resulting logistical problems.

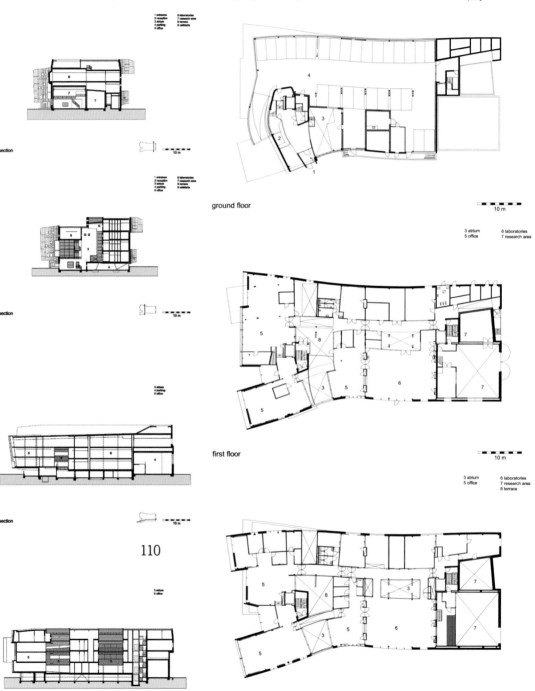

1 entrance
2 reception
3 atrium
4 parking

section

ground floor

10 m

3 atrium
5 office
6 laboratories
7 research area

section

first floor

10 m

3 atrium
5 office
6 laboratories
7 research area
8 terrace

section

110

second floor

10 m

section

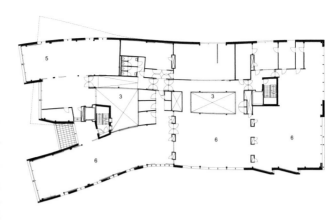

3 atrium   6 laboratories
5 office

third floor

10 m

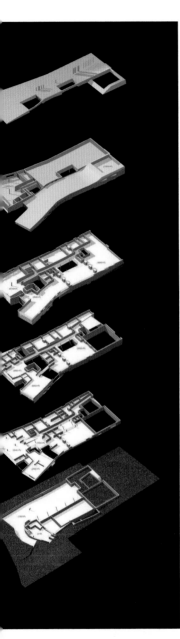

3 atrium   8 terrace
               9 cafeteria

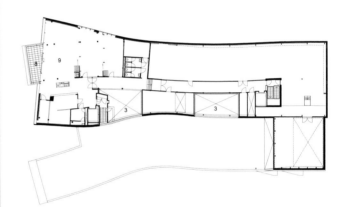

fourth floor

10 m

111

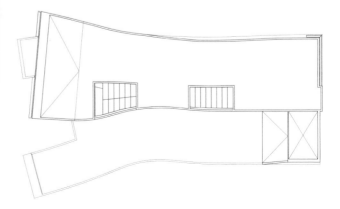

roof elevation

10 m

Many workers use the laboratory at different times of day because they have to check various test arrangements at varying moments. For these people the building is not only a terminal, but also a social environment, a place where they can exchange experiences and share events with others.

As said, the actual making of the building, with advisers and building contractors, was important as well because all left their traces in the end result. Excited about the achievement as they are, they can claim that it is a miracle of building technology.

1

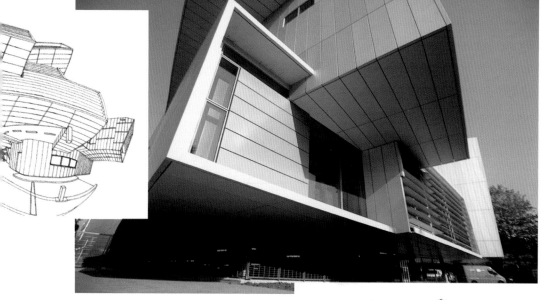

In order to bring the various realities of the different official organizations together in an overall new image and to communicate it to the public, we have used the <u>C h i m e r a</u> as inspiration.[14] The <u>C h i m e r a</u> was an image of the mythical creature from antiquity that symbolized 'Chaos'. 'Chaos', by the ancient Greeks, was seen as a positive thing, it was the primordial soup where everything was still related to everything else. There were no conflicts or collisions yet, those came into being after separate things started to emerge out of Chaos. By feeding upon this Chaos, according to their belief, life and culture could achieve revival and rejuvenation. Our <u>C h i m e r a</u>, a combination of aircraft terminal, strings, body and repair shed, represents our interpretation of the project. For us, it is a symbol of the connection between different realities that takes place in this building and a symbol of rejuvenation at the same time. In and around this capsule, people are invited to create new definitions and interpretations all the time'

(14)
CHIMERA
n Greek mythology, the Chimera Greek <u>Chímaira</u>); Latin <u>Chimae-</u> <u>a</u>) is a monstrous creature made of he parts of multiple animals. Chime- a was one of the offspring of Typhon nd Echidna and sister of such mon- ters as Cerberus and the Lernaean Hydra. Descriptions vary – some say t had the body of a goat, the tail of a snake or dragon and the head of a lion, though others say it had heads of both the goat and lion, with a snake for a tail. It is generally considered to have been female, despite the mane adorning its lion's head. All descrip- tions, however, agree that it breathed fire from one or more of its heads.' – <u>w w w . w i k i p e d i a . o r g</u>

113

Micro networks and events

A purely functional infrastructural network is like a contextless assembly line: aiming at efficiency, without room for experience or confrontation with others. It is not until micro networks originate around these infrastructural networks that a living culture is formed that is also capable of renewing itself.[15] Micro networks are different from global networks in that they connect a wide range of things with one another in a limited physical space. This enables people to choose specific ideal living conditions for themselves while remaining close and in contact with others. For some, such a condition is a chance, which causes them to have adventurous get-togethers on such junctions; for others it is the convenience of having all networks and worlds within reach. Nodes and micro networks are interactive because different people experience different realities in the same place and at the same time.[16] By mixing different people, animals and objects, their mutual relationships and connections come to occupy central stage. In the networks the interspaces and dealing spaces are also becoming active. This 'intercellular space' provides lively structures with interwoven meanings. Thus more originates than just a peaceful co-existence of differences: mutual interaction between subjects, mutual interaction between subjects and objects and mutual interaction between things.[17]

Rome in 1748

One might say that everybody lives in a different world and we all have different perspectives on reality. At weekends we each set out to our own, different familiar places to enjoy ourselves and in the evenings we watch the police series of our taste, for example set in a city like Chicago or we listen to our favourite music from Japan. We work in rational office blocks or teach children in a school, so we often think within the prejudiced rules of our own cultural worlds. Global networks connect all these physical and virtual worlds, but they seldom connect us with real people or objects. Most of the time, they only offer their own, often annoying experiences. The capsules we live or drive in, aimed at a life in splendid isolation, prevent real encounters. When driving a car, we only experience the road as if watching a video game. Even when walking from the station to the office, we have a mental capsule around us. To make real connections between people, the development of nodes and micro networks is required. Only then, real encounters and events can help to change one's otherwise frozen perspective.[18] The laboratory building in Zwijndrecht, the Jan Schaefer bridge in Amsterdam and the playground in Heijplaat, are all designed to become such nodes and micro networks.

---

(15)
MICRO-NETWORKS, NOLLI MAP OF ROME
Giovanni Battista Nolli drew beautiful maps that reveal the complicated and intimate boundaries between private and public space. The public space is not only defined by streets and squares, but also by churches, lobbies and courts of buildings.

(16)
ATOCHA STATION
The Atocha Station is considered a work of art within nineteenth century railway architecture. It was the scene of historical and social events like the departure of the Spanish troops to the War of Africa, the salute to the killed bullfighter Joselito, a background chosen by writers and the stage for a movie. The daily transfer seems to mingle reality and fiction.

(17)
DEALING SPACE
Dealing space is a space to be appropriated between parallel worlds. This interspace is never defined unequivocally, but stimulates the various users to fantasize about its possible use. It is conflicting territory. This provokes interaction and dialogue between different people and things. Dealing space can be formed in a variety of capacities (patio, square, street, bridge, room, balcony etc.) and may be situated inside as well as outside buildings.

(18)
EVENT
An event takes place when things start to happen. For example when reading a good book that changes your view on the world. Or participating in a live music event, feeling the rhythm and becoming one with all others. That is an event, because it changes your mental capsule. I use the word event to indicate the period of time in which one's world is no longer predictable. When the shell of your capsule is broken, so to say. After a real event, albeit an everyday event, one's identity has changed, slightly, or dramatically. The real problem of a capsular society is that it slows down the pace of events and the changes that come with it. According to Baudrillard, in the nineties of the last century, 'events were on strike' Baudrillard, Jean, Illusion of the end or Strike of Events (L'Illusion de la fin; ou La grève des évenements) (Paris: Galilee, 1992)

Nodes and micro networks can be made in numerous different ways and can lead to many different kinds of events. There are still many situations where it is possible to stimulate the events of everyday life and the small changes that come with it. If it is possible to develop real public spaces that do not fall victim to the dominance of cars or commerce, it is possible to make vibrant inter-spaces between capsules like apartments, offices, ateliers, shops and restaurants.[19] This inter-space creates many opportunities for accidental encounters, for temporary use as living room, veranda, theatre, forum or playground. Such places can be called 'dealing spaces' because they are real inter-spaces: there is no dominant function like traffic or commerce. People have to negotiate how to use such a place.[20] Films like <u>Lost in translation</u>, <u>Smoke</u> and <u>Taxi</u> show the potential of these and many other places where the everyday experience with its unexpected events and exchanges can survive.

Pressure cookers for making connections are 'heterotopias'. A zoological garden, a good film, a library, a theatre, a music festival, art and an entertainment park, are all examples of micro network nodes but they are secluded places at the same time. When entering such a place, one has to perform certain rituals to get detached from everyday life. They are places or virtual places that represent, or connect to, different networks at the same time. Their only purpose seems to be to connect people and their different worlds in order to achieve change. Michel Foucault described heterotopias as places where society unconsciously organizes change through ritualized 'events' in everyday life and popular culture. How this takes place and what connections people actually make, is unpredictable.[21]

(19)
NON-EVENT

Not everything that you experience is an event. A fake experience, or the feeling of an event, can be the result of a deliberate hypnotization from the side of a producer who wants to sell something, like in a shopping centre, a mediocre B-movie or entertainment park. In such a case, the shopping experience is mainly aimed at straight-forward consumption, so probably not too many new neural connections are made in your brain. Their effect on the contrary is to stimulate you into repeating the same thought time and again, causing neural highways and obsessive disorders as a result.

According to Rem Koolhaas, non-events were everywhere because capitalism turns everything into a spectacle. And he may at least partially be right. Non-events not only occur in contemporary commercial films and entertainment parks. Hypnotizing the audience goes back to Richard Wagner's opera house at Bayreuth. Before Richard Wagner, going to the opera or listening to a concert was mainly a social event. The audience was loud, talking to each other, and not paying too much attention. The event included everything around the music proper. Seeing and being seen by people, talking and drinking, all was as important as enjoying the life performance. This changed dramatically with the introduction of Wagner's opera house. There the music players were withdrawn from sight by the introduction of a lowered orchestra pit. The illusion of the play became the most important issue. Even special effects and tricks were introduced and it was

a key issue to eliminate all visibility of the technology needed. The public was made to feel and react as one super organism. At the same time, the music was used to overwhelm the audience in order to make it believe the myths and fairytales. This was an important reason behind the vehement attacks by his former admirer and philosopher Friedrich Nietzsche, who preferred a lighter approach to a music event and a more active audience. Baudrillard, Jean, <u>Illusion of the End or Strike of Events</u>, <u>L'Illusion de la fin: ou La gréve des évenements</u> (Paris: Galilee, 1992)

Nietzsche, Friedrich, <u>Nietzsche contra Wagner</u> 1895

Koolhaas, Rem and Bruce Mau: <u>S,M,L,XL</u> (Rotterdam: 010 Publishers, 1995)

(20)
THOMAS HIRSCHHORN

A beautiful example of an event in inter-space can be experienced in works and events of the contemporary Swiss artist, Thomas Hirschhorn. In the year 2002, at <u>Documenta Kassel</u>, he participated with a work, or, maybe a better description, an ongoing event, called 'The Bataille Pavillion'. It was not situated in the <u>Documenta</u> exhibition spaces, but in a temporary pavilion in a courtyard of an immigrant neighbourhood. Boys from that area helped him to build a shed that was used as radio studio, lounge bar and (porn) library, with books by Bataille and other philosophers, but also a whole range of porn magazines. Next to it was a sausage and pizza stand. The public was brought to the place

by worn-out, second hand Mercedes. In the pavilion, everyday discussion and lectures took place, radio programmes were broadcasted. It was a real mix of high and low culture, with real people hanging around and participating. Everything from building the shed, dealing with local people, the discussions, going there by Mercedes Benz, and even eating the sausages, was considered part of the event.

(21)
HETEROTOPIA

In one of his seminal texts, Michel Foucault described how every society creates places where the everyday order of space and time is lacking. In the Greek polis, for example, the theatre, the acropolis (city of the Gods) and the necropolis (city of the dead) were such places. In other cultures there are bathhouses, cruise ships, holiday resorts and the Internet. In heterotopias, as these places are called, people are not carpenter, politician, lawyer or architect but merely participants. Visiting such places and participating in the events that take place there, enables people to postpone the pursuit of their personal interest and change their perspective on the world, because their daily habit of trying to control life, health, hierarchy, trade and achievement, is temporarily suspended. Events in heterotopias are often combined with music and poetry, because these art forms have a strong power to connect where normal language tends to strengthen differences.

A strong example of heterotopia is a theatre. One can watch the scenes and witness events on an artificial

platform in the compressed time of the play. Scenes are displayed that represent faraway places and narrators and singers bring past events and remote battlefields to the stage. Participating in the event, people go through forgotten emotions and for get who they used to be.

Foucault, Michel, 'Of Other Spaces, heterotopias' (1967) published in: <u>Architecture /Mouvement/ Continuité</u> (October, 1984), tr. Jay Miskowiec.

Popular films, books and even amusement parks can also function as a node or micro network where changes take place. Consciously or unconsciously, the goal of designers and scenario writers is often to create 'events'; moments where people who witness a play or a film forget, or lose control of their perspective on the worlds they normally live in. They often want people to actively participate in their 'events'. 'Events' break the 'blasé' attitude we normally assume in commercial places.[22] This results in stress release: the 'event' relieves the spirit of the audience and makes new connections between different people, worlds or spheres possible. All this is achieved by the controllable effects of montage, shock, disorientation and suspense.

Scenario writers and film directors often employ themes and specific theatrical techniques, and powerful mythological narrative that everybody is familiar with. Each generation before us interpreted previous versions of mythology and theatre and made some changes to adapt themes, narratives and techniques to the experiences of their own time.

Internet and television can, just like film and literature, be an important part of the ongoing tradition of creating un-thought-of connections and events. They also play with those age-old themes and even though we cannot predict the exact effects, their artificial adventures have a tremendous impact on our lives. So it is a natural thing to use these powerful connecting devises and appropriate their architectural and mythological themes and techniques for making cities and buildings into a vibrant environment for the everyday life of people and things.

In our office we re-appropriate the artificial adventures with the same purpose: to create events that stimulate unpredictable experiences. Just like many filmmakers, we use the opportunities of chance encounters with 'others' to relieve the spirit and to generate new connections and cultural change.

The destiny of a voyage is less interesting than travelling itself. When dealing with the strange world of networks, one of our sources of inspiration may be Big Thunder Mountain Railroad in Disneyland: a little train passing through a mountain. A rollercoaster thundering through miniature mountain scenery, all the time giving you the idea that you are about to bump your head, or some criminal is going to attack you. When we are making plans for infrastructure, it is a notion of event and adventure that we have in mind. We believe that everyone enjoys driving through canyons and along twisting roads in a cabriolet, because you really smell the mountains, feel the asphalt and experience the sublime landscape. We also believe this experience can be introduced in micro networks that function on a totally different scale.[23]

117

---

(22)
HEGEL
Recently, the Fenomenology of Spirit, a philosophical work of Hegel, has been used in the contemporary context of the discussions surrounding the multicultural society, to break into the ongoing promotion of ethnicity and identity. In this very complex book, Hegel describes the way a person, or society develops knowledge about the world and oneself, through encounters and confrontations with others' or other bodies of knowledge. When such encounters take place, the other disturbs a person's existing beautiful image of the world'. After an initial period of unhappiness however, the result of such encounters is either a refusal to change one's image of the world (resulting in scepticism, irony or

sarcasm), or it ends in creating a new personal image of the world and even a sense of liberation and happiness. After that, the whole cycle repeats itself timelessly. This basic idea was later elaborated by other writers who included the idea that even language itself could act as 'other'.

Suggested reading: Hegel (Phenomenology of Spirit), Baudelaire (Le Flaneur), Sartre, Saussure, Jakobson, Freud, Lacan

(23)
BATAILLE
Another version of the concept of an event was described by Georges Bataille. For Bataille, prehistoric life consisted of two different impulses. One was a longing for health, oneness and harmony, but since this also caused

stress and solitude, the other was a longing for becoming part of every-thing, ending in a longing for (near) self-destruction or 'small death'. This impulse was exercised in ecstatic (ecstatic: lit: out of the being) rites. In Bataille's eyes, mankind had lost the appetite for the ritualized Dionysiac event, resulting in a constant search for health and safety. Time and again, this would lead to catastrophic wars, like World War I, or other violent events, where the opposite of total destruction was achieved. In his own work, quite the opposite of classical beauty can be seen. He was constantly trying to find the connection between art, the sacred and the violent.

Other writers used different words for basically the same opposition; the classical versus the mannerist

or the classical versus the sublime. 'The sublime' is a specific kind of aesthetic principle that many artists used and developed over the ages. It is not based on principles of classical beauty and human control, but aimed at creating a sense of horror and terror that is both repelling and attractive. The canyons in the Alps can be seen as an example of sublime beauty. Friedrich Nietzsche, used the terms Apollinian and Dionysiac. The presence of gangs in many countries suggests that the main problem of the capsular society is the absence of capsular the popular impulse to eliminate the Dionysiac or the Sublime, resulting in drug abuse and drive-by shootings.

Suggested reading: Bataille, Georges, The Blue of noon tr. Le Blue du ciel (1985).

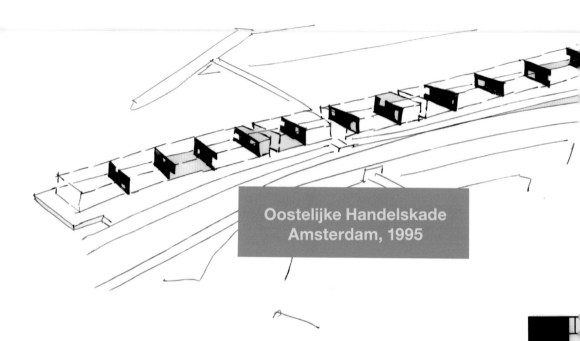

Oostelijke Handelskade
Amsterdam, 1995

Oostelijke Handelskade – a vertical city

In the same period we were working on the bridge to Java Isle, we also participated in a multiple order for the Oostelijke Handelskade in Amsterdam. A strip of land was available of 60 metres deep, 35 metres high and 1,600 metres long, with the river IJ on the northern side and a busy road and railway on the south side. The old warehouses on the waterfront had meanwhile been claimed by squatters as well as by the National Trust. On the side of the road, the main issues were e.g. noise pollution combined with a view of the skyline of downtown Amsterdam. The assignment within this context was to investigate the possibility of realizing houses in a high density of the same quality as those in the city centre or outside the city, with gardens and outside spaces. In fact, the houses not only had to compete with the suburban houses pattern, but also with the sense of freedom people experience in the cluttered fringes of urban areas, where they keep poultry, pimp cars, store their caravans and organize parties in old sheds.[24]

118

(24)
NEURAL NETWORKS
Happiness seems to be closely related to neural processes in the brain. Micro-networks in the brain are called neural networks. Learning in biological systems deals with adaptations in synaptic connections between neurons. To challenge your brain by dealing with new situations and problems, seems to be very healthy for your brain, whereas the lack of new information or impulses seems to cause a rapid deteriorization. Repeating the same strain of thoughts over and over again can cause the construction of a 'neural highway', reinforcing that same thought: eat, eat, vomit, vomit, (obesities) or I am ugly, I am ugly, the world is going to pieces, etcetera. So, plain is going to crash, it is good to regularly experience life changing events and the changes of perspective that come with it.

A

B

F

G

DOORSNEDEN   schaal 1/2000

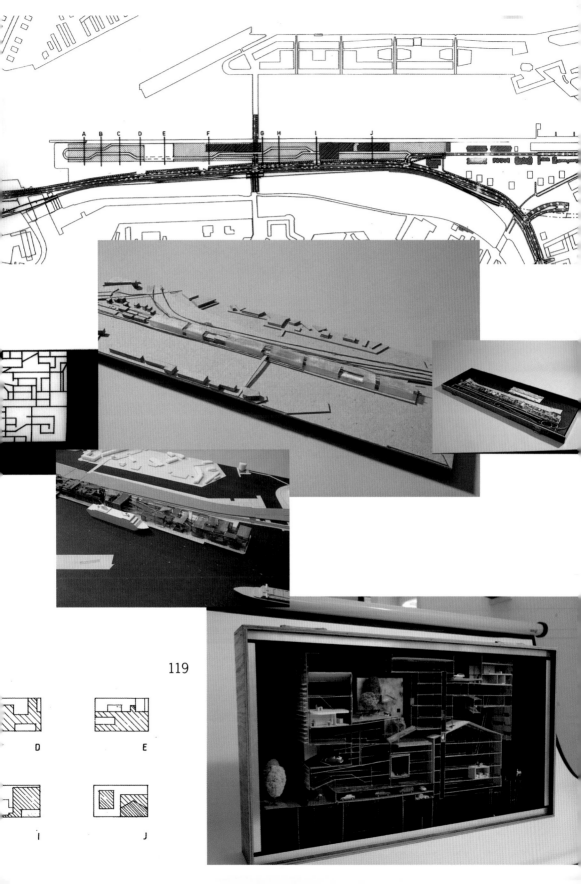

119

In our plan the isolated situation of the area was not ignored, but came to occupy central stage, by proposing an almost autonomous, stacked city in a volume that completely filled the available strip. The filling-in of this volume was based on maximum tolerance for chance during the development phase. For this purpose, the volume was split up in slices with a length of about 150 metres each, all with their own sectional views and informal design rules. On this the various property developers could base their choices. The product as a whole was to become a c a d a v r e   e x q u i s, because the developers were only given information about the mutual points of contact.[25] The design rules had not been made to check the ideal final result, but to encourage a creative process. As with the music composer John Cage who used chance as a seminal composing devise, the idea was that the directions in the score would time and again invite a different execution.[26]

(25)
CADAVRE EXQUIS

In a drawing called a c a d a v r e   e s - q u i s, a strange picture is made by the efforts of different people who cannot see each other's drawing, because the paper is folded. The only clues you have, where to continue the drawing, are tiny lines that cross the folds between the different sections.

(26)
JOHN CAGE

'John Milton Cage (September 5, 1912 – August 12, 1992) was an American experimental music composer, writer and visual artist. He is most widely known for his 1952 composition 4' 3 3 ", whose three movements are performed without playing a single note. Cage was an early composer of what he called "chance music" (and what others have decided to label aleatoric music) – music where some elements are left to be decided by chance; he is also well known for his non-standard use of musical instruments and his pioneering exploration of electronic music. His works were sometimes controversial, but he is generally regarded as one of the most important composers of his era, especially in his raising questions about the definition of music. John Cage put Zen Buddhist beliefs into practice through music. He described his music as "purposeless play", but "this play is an affirmation of life – not an attempt to bring order out of chaos, nor to suggest improvements in creation, but simply to wake up to the very life we are living, which is so excellent once one gets one's mind and desires out of the way and lets it act of its own accord".'- http://en.wikipedia. org/wiki/John cage

The infrastructure was part of the project: cycle paths, footpaths, roads and tramways. In each section connecting the different segments these elements were allotted a particular place. Specific factors were incorporated such as sun, view, noise and wind. Connecting these sections was an important precondition for every property developer. In addition, incidents had been included in the different segments, such as 'this is a warehouse occupied by squatters that you cannot simply throw out', which was something the developers had to bear in mind.

In our role as designers of a city, we could not predict which actual functions would be developed in what particular place, so we focused our efforts on the process, the internal infrastructure and the realization of open internal spaces, the so-called interspaces, as key elements for obtaining a good quality of life. These spaces were connected by a shared internal infrastructure. Squares, parks, meadows, boulevards, bike tracks, slopes and bridges started to take form. One could walk, hang around, drive, park, cycle and stroll. The infrastructure ran through the volume in different layers, and in the sections you could find things like an alpine meadow with cows, an annex of Artis Zoo, a music studio and many other elements, together forming a busy city. The infrastructure was not only used to connect pleasant places in a safe manner. The linear spaces and moving elements were all part of the events of life in this vertical city. On the whole, it resembled a modern version of the hanging gardens of Babylon.[27]

(27)
HANGING GARDENS OF BABYLON
When Nebuchadnezzar's wife Amytis complained she was homesick and longing for the mountains of her childhood, Nebuchadnezzar promised her to bring the mountains to Mesopotamia.

The different projects were unified by a homogeneous treatment of the facade, with the possibility for the specific differences to shine through. It was like everybody would live in an enormous biosphere, an organic palace, or, to put it differently, we have rolled up the entire pattern of organized suburbia and informal fringes like a sushi roll and moulded it into one single building mass.'

123

**Industry and living, Cruquiusweg
Amsterdam, 2000**

park

entreedek

P

P

P

bedrijfsruimte

124

Cruquiusweg – living in a power plant

Creating density after a century of obsession with suburbanization is a theme that runs throughout all our works. The advantages of density are numerous: there are social benefits, environmental, economical and physical, to name but a few. In October 1999 we were asked to make a proposal for an inner city industrial site, our client could buy the location from a wholesale wine trader who occupied the site. We faced several conflicting issues in developing our scheme. On one side we were facing a very attractive waterfront, but it was oriented towards the north, on the other side we faced a noisy industrial site. Also the land was extremely expensive, so we had to propose an intensive programme. The city council wanted jobs for low skilled, instead of apartments for the rich. So we made a combination of everything. Spaces for industry and small businesses on the lower levels facing the industrial site were combined with a parking garage, supermarket, fitness, day care centre and indoor harbour, with a public park on top, as an extension of the public walkway over the quay. Along the waterfront and on top of the park, apartments were planned – in vertical slabs to allow the sun to filter through – thirty percent social housing and seventy percent commercial housing, as we are used to in the Netherlands.

125

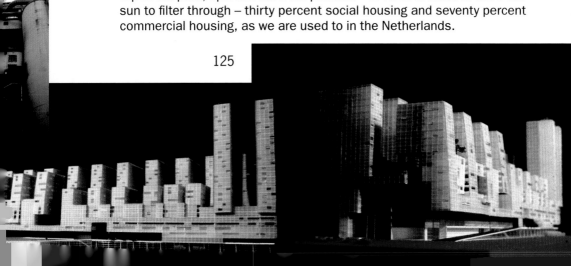

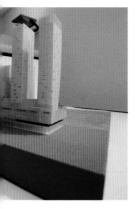

127

Kooiplein – a gathering of hybrid buildings and networks

Small everyday encounters and events were aimed at in a project for the redevelopment of a part of the city of Leiden. In the case of previous projects we were engaged in urban development all right, but the Kooiplein project was in fact the first time that our office stepped in to deal with the networks of the urban conurbation. What we have here is a block for senior citizens with a busy road on one side and a small shopping centre on the other. Currently these two are connected by a narrow and poky cycle tunnel – the traffic is too heavy to cross the road safely. The Town Council's idea was to direct all through traffic through a tunnel. This was supposed to improve the bicycle and pedestrian connection between the inner city, an isolated park and the suburbs further away. When we got started, there turned out to be more problems and the assignment became more wide-ranging. The Kooiplein was to become a new centre for multicultural north Leiden so that life in the city was in a better position to compete with the suburbs. The new tunnel had to ensure that the formerly isolated park became the leisure centre of the bigger neighbourhood.

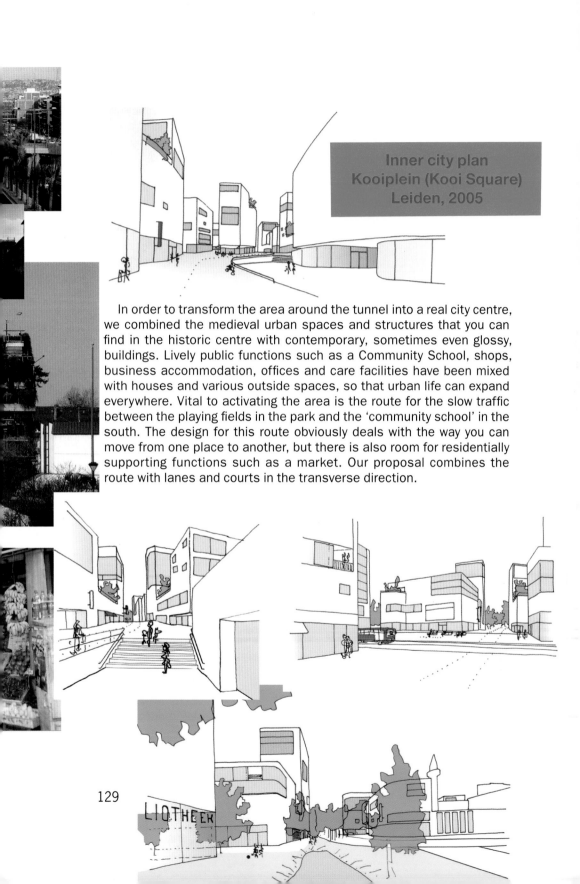

In order to transform the area around the tunnel into a real city centre, we combined the medieval urban spaces and structures that you can find in the historic centre with contemporary, sometimes even glossy, buildings. Lively public functions such as a Community School, shops, business accommodation, offices and care facilities have been mixed with houses and various outside spaces, so that urban life can expand everywhere. Vital to activating the area is the route for the slow traffic between the playing fields in the park and the 'community school' in the south. The design for this route obviously deals with the way you can move from one place to another, but there is also room for residentially supporting functions such as a market. Our proposal combines the route with lanes and courts in the transverse direction.

129

The building blocks of the new centre consist in hybrid building blocks. These have a ground floor for shops, commercial activities, studios, amenities and hotels and restaurants, with a wide variety of houses on a higher level. Important items are also the collective spaces, roof terraces and courtyard gardens that offer room for relaxation and recreation. Underneath one of the blocks is a mega supermarket that connects directly with the underground car parks.

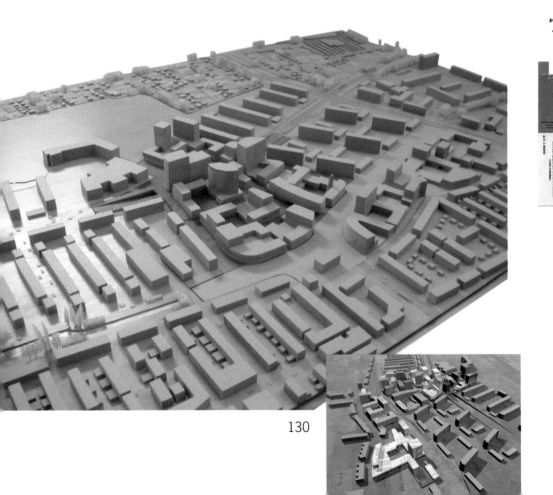

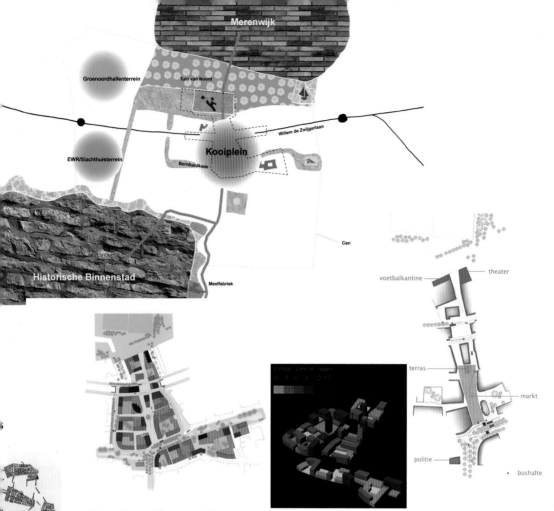

The plan offers a different way to experience the space per different kind of traffic. Motorists see a surveyable neighbourhood where it is easy to get their bearings. The pedestrians experience a picturesque series of squares as found in historic inner cities. The buildings represent a mixture of various cultures, in the same way as their residents who come from all over the world and have meanwhile developed all kinds of hybrid cultures.[28] Traditional modernist buildings are side to side with brick, glass, orthogonal or distorted buildings or combinations thereof. In this way a natural aggregate originates that reflects everyday reality as it has come into being over the years. As all kinds of different elements are situated close to one another, different generations can also live close to one another. At any moment in time, different people use different networks within the same fabric.

(28)
MICRO NETWORK ORGANIZATION Famous examples of local, micro-network organizations can be found in Mumbai, where people living in shantytowns are extremely successful in organizing efficient laundry systems, garbage recycling and food production, even though nobody seems to be in charge. Shantytowns in general seem to have almost perfectly working Cradle-to-Cradle systems, turning them into interesting examples for the construction of zero energy, or energy producing cities. The 'Core Hospital' concept, described later in this book, aims at comparably positive, environmental effects.

131

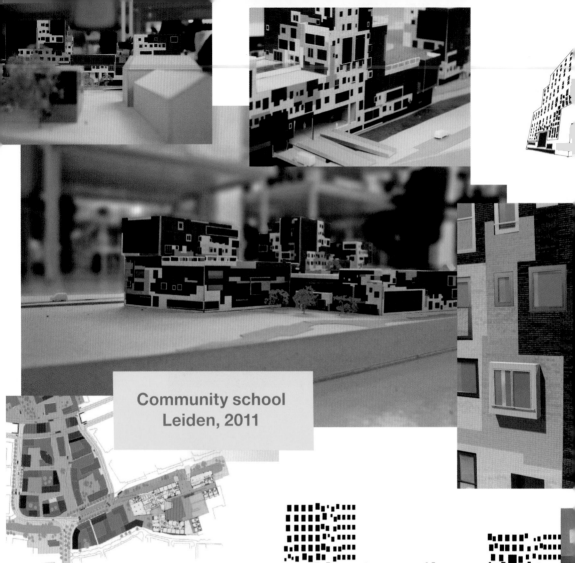

**Community school
Leiden, 2011**

132

Community school Kooiplein – the city as school

In the 'community school' four different primary schools are combined with all kinds of local amenities such as a public library, health care facilities and a cultural centre. This project is going to be the first to improve not only the spatial qualities of the neighbourhood, but also its social tissue. The combination of schools brings children from different ethnic background to the same place. Together with all other activities in the building they create a cultural node that supports social life in the neighbourhood. The central space in this building can be used as cinema, playground, bar, convention centre, or theatre. All apartments, the library, the schools and all other functions share the same camouflaged outer skin, whereas the interior is conceived as 'miniature city in a building'. The school's play area is part of the court structure of the Kooiplein area. In this way the various amenities form a structure with other activities in the neighbourhood.

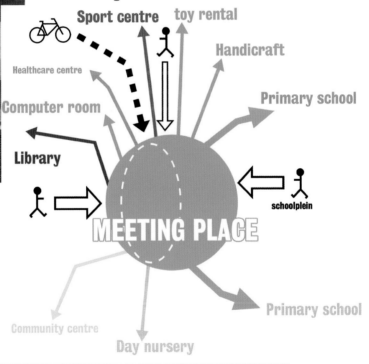

Sport centre · toy rental · Handicraft · Healthcare centre · Computer room · Primary school · Library · schoolplein · MEETING PLACE · Community centre · Day nursery · Primary school

133

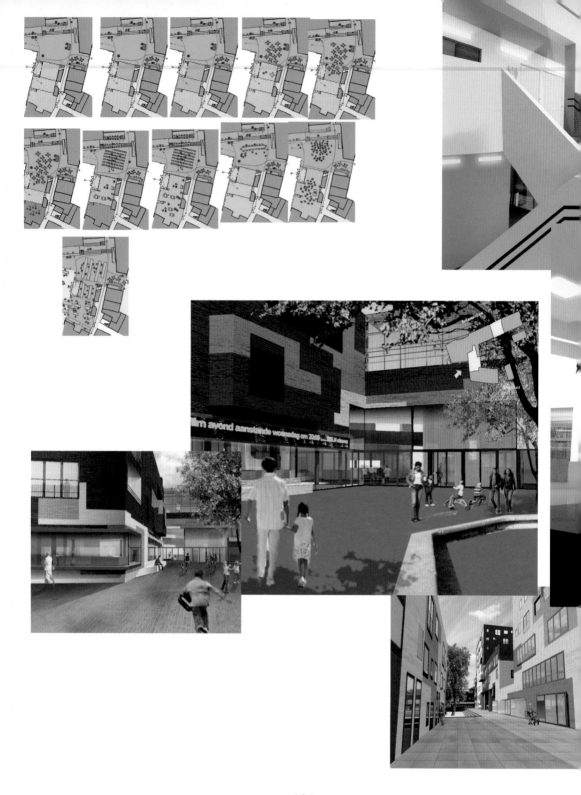

Dockroad area IJmuiden – a crowd of buildings

Shortly before the Kooiplein in Leiden, we made a development plan for the city of IJmuiden. As port of Amsterdam, the city was heavily bombed in World War II. Currently the post war city centre is located far from the seaside. The harbour outside of the seawall occupies the front row, immediately followed by suburbs behind the dike. The city's economy is struggling because production and shipping moved elsewhere. Only marginal businesses remain.

Dockroad area IJmuiden, 2003

136

137

To revive the city's economy we proposed a development plan that focuses on the introduction of mixed use in this part of the metropolitan area of Amsterdam: tourism and creative industry could be mixed with other businesses and apartments, creating a lively harbour front. Our proposal was conceived as a viral strategy, a first step, aiming at further transformations in harbour and suburbs later on. Creating density in this area made it possible to give part of the client's land back to nature. Dunes could be redeveloped for nature where worn-out industrial sheds had spoiled the landscape for a long time.

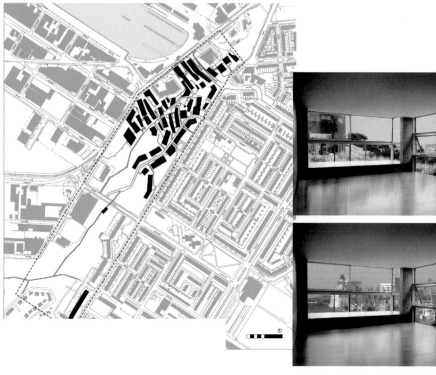

138

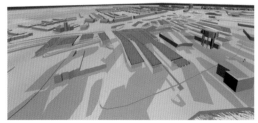

According to the directions, no houses could be built on the bottom seven metres of the area outside the dike, as the statistics said that there is a once in a thousand year chance of a flood. For that reason we had to find other functions for that spot, a mayor opportunity to turn IJmuiden into Amsterdam's recreational harbour front and this lower part – with its shops, bars, restaurants, ateliers and workshops – into the vibrant basis of our design. We housed car parks in an extension of the dike that could be reached by way of side streets and we turned the area into a pedestrian's paradise.

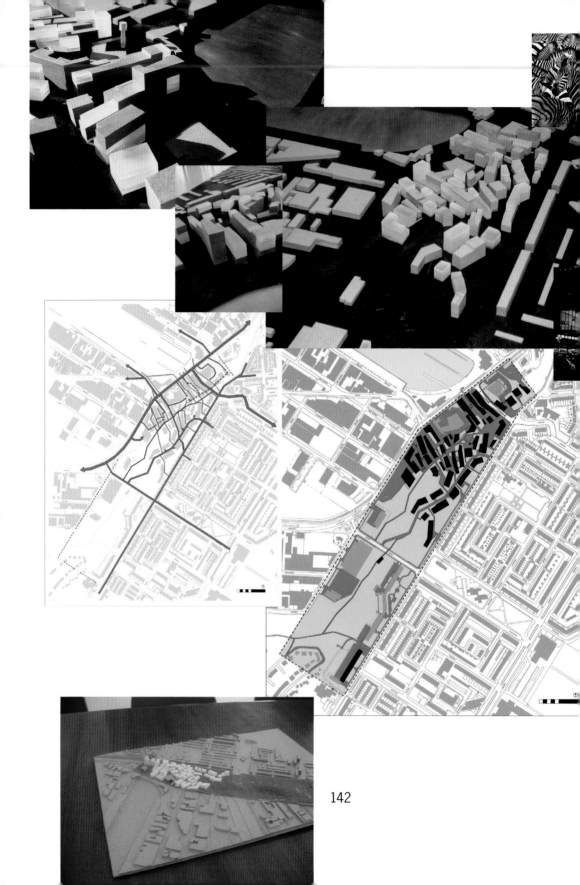

142

The entire plan was one big pedestrian area like the Wallen in Amsterdam or Soho in Hong Kong. A fabric of inside spaces, outside spaces, routes and squares spread over the area. The streets were not straight, but ran in curved lines between harbour and dunes. When one would walk in the direction of the harbour, one could see the reflection of the water at the end, but the direct view of the water was suspended until one would turn the corner. Thus an urban interior came into being, but also a direct connection with the dunes. The difference in level between the seawall and the quay was bridged by means of stairs, escalators and lifts integrated into the same urban tissue. Each building developed its own scale and shape. The buildings look alike, but are not the same. By mixing all life functions in different sizes, big, medium and small, and all ranges of income and lifestyle, lively structures and a dazzling entirety were achieved. The resulting plan looks a bit like a curious herd of buildings pouncing on the harbour. With all its seminal ideas it can be regarded as predecessor of many of our urban development plans.

143

Core Hospital – the city as hospital

A totally different and architecturally more elaborated example of how mixing functions and infrastructure into micro networks can be used to stimulate life in urban areas has been worked out in the project Future Hospital. This design shows how a hospital can benefit from urban functions in its vicinity and how the urban culture can benefit from the presence of a hospital. Such an interrelationship can in due course be mutually beneficial.

Personally I have an aversion to hospitals when I think of the way they have been built in the Netherlands these last few decades. They are often technocratic, vast and are situated outside towns and cities amidst extensive car parks. You get stuck in traffic jams on your way to the visiting hours and if you are there for an examination or treatment, more often than not you have to wait for hours in a variety of ugly waiting rooms. As part of a competition for the hospital of the future we have been thinking about a new concept for such hospitals.

By relying on the network-organized supply for certain parts of society's healthcare programme, it is possible to reduce the size of a hospital building drastically.[29] The original assignment took its departure from a hospital of 42,000 m² for 150,000 residents. In our proposal this was translated into a core hospital of 21,000 m² of core functions only. The other half was split up into parts that were not necessarily required to be in the hospital's direct vicinity. They could even be offered by separate companies, allowing the hospital to focus entirely on high quality cure.

The concept was enabled by the emergence of microsurgery, because it causes a sharp reduction in healing time and the need for nursing. Also, cheaper diagnostic equipment and the rise of tele-diagnostics and ICT networks make decentralization possible. The development of these technologies will further reduce the amount of visitors and the length of a stay in a hospital in the future.[30]

This allows for a 'mean and lean' hospital concept that is so compact that it fits into any average building block of a European city. It is not a spreading technocratic structure for which four city blocks must be reserved. In addition to the hospital, houses or hotels could also be included in the building block. From an economic point of view, this is also an interesting concept; the buildings can easily be hived off or sold in the future, because they represent a high value in an urban context. The concept is flexible and nevertheless perfectly fitting.

(29)
NETWORK ORGANIZATION
This refers to a 'mean and lean' business model with a 'just in time' delivery from suppliers that take part in the network organization of a producer of, for example, cars. More and more industries can be taken as good examples of such organizations, which generally have a low operating cost structure. Check Toyota's website!

(30)
MICROSURGERY OR MINIMAL INVASIVE SURGERY
Minimal invasive surgery has created a revolution in surgery. Microsurgery takes only minor incisions in the body and allows for a rapid recovery. Through Minimal invasive surgery, many operations can nowadays be performed in day surgery. This popular technique saves a lot of time and money and creates the opportunity to cut the size of the hospitals sharply.

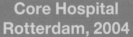

Core Hospital
Rotterdam, 2004

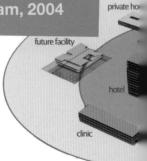

private ho

future facility

hotel

clinic

The idea underlying the <u>c o r e   h o s p i t a l</u> concept is that many of the functions usually housed inside the hospital are in fact out of place there, whereas others should be given a place inside. A physiotherapist for example might as well take up residence with a health club and office space can be made almost everywhere. Even big parts of outpatient departments function better when distributed among neighbourhoods. It would save a lot of traffic and these decentralized centres would be very beneficial for children and older people living there.

On the other hand, in a vibrant city centre, a hotel next to the hospital can serve tourists and businessmen and at the same offer a flexible and hospitable annex to the hospital. The hotel reception desk can receive people who come into the hospital for day treatment and the hospital can use the rooms, the hospitality of the hotel and its kitchen.

In our design, the hospital shops are situated on the edge of the marketplace next to it; they are both accessible from the hospital and from the city. Visitors, passers-by and patients can use the florist, the pub and the cinema alike. Thus the ground floor is part of city life, whereas the medical functions begin on the first floor. For this higher-level part of the design we drew inspiration from medieval monasteries, where you often see a combination of serene courtyard gardens with cloisters and rooms efficiently grouped around them. These spaces create a wellness atmosphere that reduces stress and stimulates healing.

The most essential aspect of the plan is that it is flexible and commonplace, for the building is part of city life. Nowadays, with ever-shorter recuperation times, an urban environment for the hospital is more natural than the green setting outside the city that was more usual in the old days. This, incidentally, gives an entirely new meaning to the traditional notion of <u>h e a l i n g   e n v i r o n m e n t</u>. The very awareness that one only has to stay in hospital for a short while, at the same time remaining part of the urban society, stimulates one's recovery.

Even though this is a very efficient and flexible solution to reintegrate the hospital in the city tissue, an inner city location also offers limitations regarding growth. So making a building complex like this with a more or less fixed maximum size is possible because it is a general hospital, focussing on acute care and common diseases only. For patients that require very complicated specialist treatment, the network offers university hospitals that are specialized in and even require complicated cases.

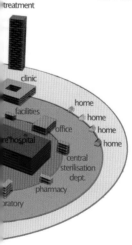

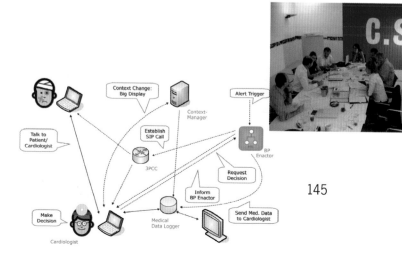

145

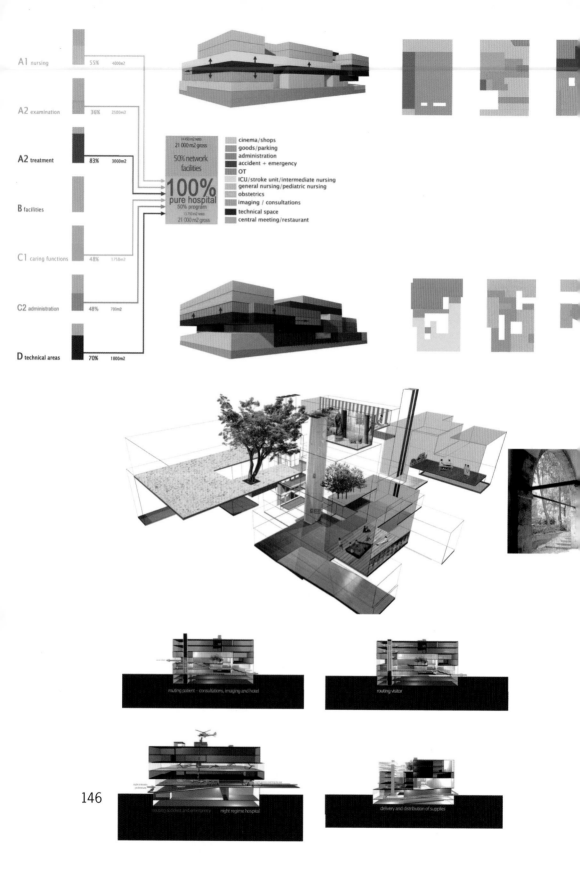

A1 nursing — 55% — 4000m2

A2 examination — 36% — 2500m2

A2 treatment — 83% — 3000m2

B facilities

C1 caring functions — 48% — 1750m2

C2 administration — 48% — 700m2

D technical areas — 70% — 1800m2

(4 450 m2 netto)
21 000 m2 gross
50% network
facilities
100%
pure hospital
50% program
13 700 m2 netto
21 000 m2 gross

cinema/shops
goods/parking
administration
accident + emergency
OT
ICU/stroke unit/intermediate nursing
general nursing/pediatric nursing
obstetrics
imaging / consultations
technical space
central meeting/restaurant

routing patient – consultations, imaging and hotel

routing visitor

routing accident and emergency   night regime hospital

delivery and distribution of supplies

146

Stradins University Hospital – the hospital as city

The idea of the core hospital was further developed in our proposal for the Paul Stradins University Hospital of Riga, the capital of the Republic of Latvia. The main design assignment was to create a master plan for the future development and extension of this culturally and medically important university hospital. At the same time, the area should be developed to become a major park and leisure centre for the inhabitants of the neighbourhood. Complicating the assignment were the beautiful Jugendstil buildings of the existing hospital on the site. They were to be given a new life with economically feasible functions that would contribute to the quality of life in the hospital, the park and the neighbourhood.

147

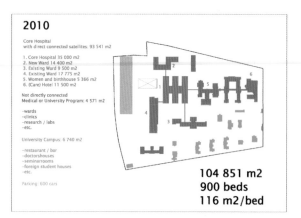

2010

Core Hospital
with direct connected satellites: 93 541 m2

1. Core Hospital 35 000 m2
2. New Ward 14 400 m2
3. Existing Ward 9 500 m2
4. Existing Ward 17 775 m2
5. Women and birthhouse 5 366 m2
6. (Care) Hotel 11 500 m2

Not directly connected
Medical or University Program: 4 571 m2

–wards
–clinics
–research / labs
–etc.

University Campus: 6 740 m2

–restaurant / bar
–doctorshouses
–seminarrooms
–foreign student houses
–etc.

Parking: 600 cars

104 851 m2
900 beds
116 m2/bed

Core Hospital
Stradins University hospital
Riga, 2005

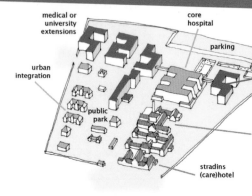

medical or university extensions

core hospital

parking

urban integration

public park

stradins (care)hotel

2020

Core Hospital
with direct connected satellites: 120 166 m2

1. Core Hospital 35 000 m2
2. New Ward 14 400 m2
3. Existing Ward 9 500 m2
4. New Ward 14 400 m2
5. Women and birthhouse 5 366 m2
6. (Care) Hotel 11 500 m2
7. Lab / R&D 15 000 m2
8. Extensions Core hospital 15 000 m2

Not directly connected
Medical or University Program: 45 000 m2

–wards
–clinics
–research / labs
–etc.

University Campus: 6740 m2

–restaurant / bar
–doctorshouses
–seminarrooms
–foreign student houses
–etc.

Parking: 1000 cars

171 905 m2
700 beds
245 m2/bed

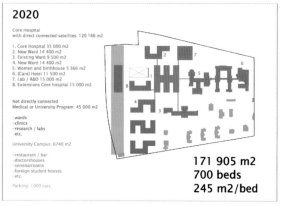

In general I think it is a good idea to try to combine such totally different ambitions. After all, when the hospital is situated in a nice environment and many people like to live in its vicinity, pedestrian connections can be used to connect different destinies, stimulating health and saving the environment. Also, all kinds of urban functions may profit economically from different types of clients such as inhabitants and visitors of the park and the neighbourhood and people living and working in the hospital. Of course these facilities also make working and living in the area more attractive. Which is again good for the economy of the hospital and the market value of redundant buildings.

148

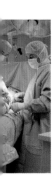

Making one building containing all the hospital functions in one compact core does not function well in a university hospital. Departments also need spaces for students and departments grow with their research and domestic demand. To allow for maximum flexibility, we concentrated on bringing all the technologically complicated functions together in a technologically advanced, flexible core. All other buildings with temporary functions like wards, laboratories and offices were separated from this nucleus and situated around it, to create a pavilion type university hospital. Only bridges and tunnels were used to connect to the diagnostic and intensive care units. This way the walkways of the park could extend to all extremes of the area and into the neighbourhood.

Sportplaza Mercator
Amsterdam, 2006

Sportplaza Mercator – city in a cave

Some orders evoke an irrepressible desire to leave the classic architectural repertoire behind and try to fit in with the language of the street instead. Sportplaza Mercator reminds one of an amusement park and fortification at the same time. It is reminiscent of the world of the James Bond films – where the bad guys hide in subterranean complexes – and that of <u>The Thunderbirds</u>, where the heroes live underground. In mass culture a cave is neither good nor bad, it is an ambiguous space where these qualities blend.[31]

(31)
Check the internet for: Thunderbirds,
James Bond and Tora Bora

The Baarsjes, the part of the city where the sports complex is situated, is one of the best-known multicultural districts of Amsterdam, on account of its 129 nationalities. Local politicians have been trying to improve the liveability for years with a wide range of projects. With the help of investments in public buildings and public spaces and through renovation of existing buildings, the district is on its way to becoming one of the city's most attractive parts.

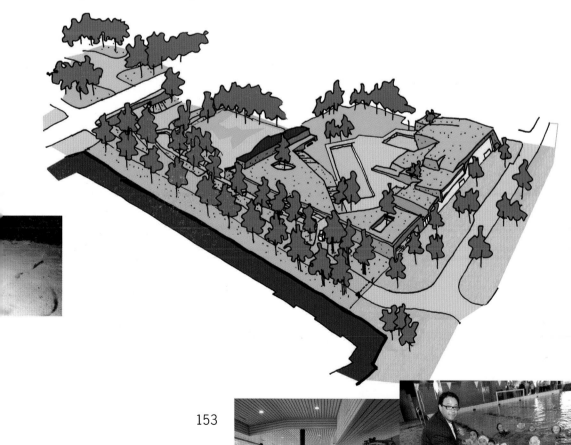

Sportplaza Mercator is a heterotopia and constitutes a junction in a fabric of local networks. Advertising has split up our society into different target groups with different needs and cultivates the contrasts between separate visual languages. By way of the icons of mass culture it is possible to readdress various communities simultaneously.

The programme for this project is a combination of a covered pool with a therapeutic bath, fitness centre, party hall, pub and a branch of Kentucky Fried Chicken. The idea is to serve the whole gamut of communities with the complex. It was designed as a miniature society, a town in a cave. There are competitive swimmers doing a few laps, partygoers, members of the fitness fraternity, parents letting their children play, rheumatics and people who prefer to just watch all the activities from the pub or the fast food restaurant. The building is full of views that make the different visitors, activities and cultures visible to one another.

The entrance has been designed like the gateway of an airport. This lobby can function as the place for a first get-together, after which everyone can use the various functions of the building as desired. We have turned the building into an i n t e r l a c e m e n t of different spaces. Each space was given its own position in the section. The competition pool is one metre below ground level and the recreational pool half a metre. The various spaces are shaped by the natural stone covering across the folded floor surfaces and walls. The linear pattern of the seams between the stone slabs accentuates the differences in height. Due to the covering of natural stone the various pools and floors call up associations with the ruins from ancient times.

156

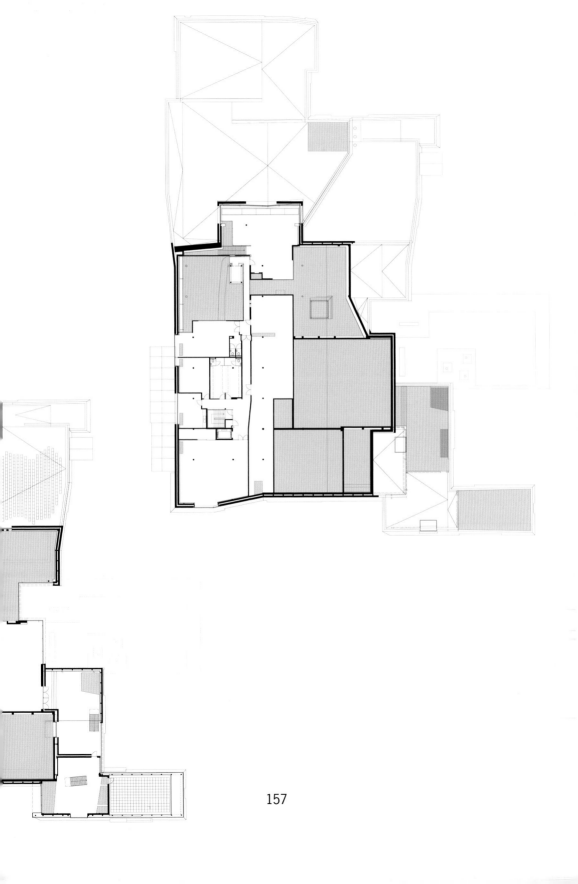

157

From the inside the roof resembles a blanket draped over the various rooms. What you see is a covering with a neutral linear pattern whose direction changes when the roof turns the corner. Similar to a striped shirt, where the direction of the pattern changes as the design dictates. Window openings are formed by slits and cracks between floor and roof. Roof, window opening and floor are interwoven in various ways and change shape all the time. Of all surface effects in the interior of the building, light is the most interactive. The artist Giny Vos created a work of light-art in the roof that refers to Plato's story of the cave. Fata Morganas of mythological pictures may pop up.

158

While the interior spaces have strong interrelationships with the various urban networks, the design of the outer shell explores the different definitions of 'skin' and 'covering'. There is no direct connection between the exterior and the interior. The differences in height between the various spaces inside, for example, can only be guessed from the outside.

159

The green roof and the elevations form one whole. To this end we have applied a cladding for which Patrick Blanc has developed the technical knowledge.[32] It is a facade that in the course of years will develop a wild overgrowth of plants, shrubs and small trees. The sharp contours of the building will disappear in the course of time and something resembling an overgrown fortress will come into being.

(32)
PATRICK BLANC
Patrick Blanc (born 1953, Paris) is a botanist, scientist for CNRS (Centre National de la Recherche Scientifique) and the inventor of the Ver-tical Garden, also known as the Living Wall.
www.verticalgardenpat-rickblanc.com

160

In some places the elevation has been treated like a skin with animal characteristics. Windows are made to look like eyes. In other places the facade has been treated like upholstering: the green front has been laid over the functions like a camouflage blanket. The building does not literally rise up from the ground; in some places it remains suspended, like a camouflaged animal. It causes the building to remain a paradox, a strange object hidden under the park.

161

Bodies, skins, herds and images

Things are not only the object of human action, but also possess a life of their own. This type of animistic vision, in which every object is a living entity, implies that the object cannot only undergo changes but also that it can cause these.[33,34] When a group of like-minded people, animals or things come together, a herd or swarm can arise. Although herds and swarms are essentially gatherings of individual entities, both often react as one unit as a result of cultural, genetic and psychological processes. Consequently, herds and swarms can also be regarded as bodies, with all the corresponding properties. Just as an enclosing skin holds the human body together, the skin for the body of the object functions as a fluid container. The skin, or rather, what we take as being the skin, ensures that the collection of individual constituents does not disintegrate into loose particles. But it does not say anything about the essence of the object. We know objects only on the basis of our own experiences, a situation that does have its restrictions. Camouflage patterns for example, connect animals to their surroundings or to other members of the herd, creating confusion by means of their virtual super-skin. But they also attract sexual attention from other members of the same species.

Objects communicate with their surroundings, just as people and animals do. Image, skin and clothing function as 'mediators'. The body enters into relationships via the skin, clothes, eyes and pores. In doing so, the body connects to its environment and renews itself.[35]

(33)
ANIMISM

In religion, the term "Animism" is used in a number of ways. Animism (from animus, or anima, mind or soul), originally means the doctrine of spiritual beings. It is often extended to include the belief that personalized, supernatural beings (or souls) endowed with reason, intelligence and volition inhabit ordinary objects as well as animate beings, and govern their existence (pantheism or animatism). More simply, the belief is that "everything is alive", "everything is conscious" or "everything has a soul". It has been further extended to mean a belief that the world is a community of living persons, only some of whom are human. It also refers to the culture or philosophy which these types of Animists live by, that is, to attempt to relate respectfully with the persons (human, rock, plant, animal, bird, ancestral, etc.) who are also members of the wider community of life.' – http://en.wikipedia.org/wiki/Animism

(34)
SHAMAN

Since it remains hard to communicate with objects, even though they seem to be living, old cultures used shamans to establish connections with the spiritual world, including the one of the objects. Shamans performed special rites to be able to listen to the messages delivered by the spirits. In many contemporary cultures this age-old function of shamans survives, albeit often under a different name. One might even say that priests, politicians and scientists are contemporary shamans, in the sense that they explain the (will of) the world and the cosmos. You can distinguish a clever shaman from a poor one, because the first always talks in riddles to allow for experiences to be mixed in with personal interpretations.

(35)
DAZZLE PAINTING

'Dazzle camouflage, also known as Razzle Dazzle or Dazzle painting, was a camouflage paint scheme used on ships, mainly during World War I. It consisted of a complex pattern of geometric shapes in contrasting colours, interrupting and intersecting each other. At first glance it seems like an unlikely form of camouflage, drawing attention to the ship rather than hiding it. Dazzle camouflage had a very specific purpose, however, which was to make it difficult to estimate the target ship's speed and heading and so disrupt the performance of the visual rangefinders used for naval artillery at the time.' – http://en.wikipedia.org/wiki/Dazzle pain

167

The lives of cities are as hard to describe as people's or nation's character or identities. Should we look at their carefully preserved historic centres that are now transformed into tourist's theme parks? Should we eliminate all later extensions, where everyday life actually takes place, from our description? Is it good to focus on some monumental buildings and historic events that might represent the supposed essence or identity of a culture? Or is the existing cultural tissue of their inhabitants their most important feature?

In spite of its image, every city is a giant collector of things, people, animals, machines, cultures and other objects. The same holds for people, who collect experiences in their brains and ancient DNA in their bodies. So, do we know more of people and objects than their outer appearance? There are simply too many mythologies and stories around people and objects to discern any essence of something.[36] The essence is a personal invention of an outsider, or, at best, a personal selection of the collection of all possible stories surrounding the object or person. You can easily change someone or something by creating a new story or perspective on the person or object.

Even a person's own brain does not really know who the person really is. It improvises constantly: if a person wants to say or do something, the brain quickly scans all information collected over the ages, for the most appropriate words, images and experiences to compare to, or deal with that specific situation, person or object.[37] There is not a direct relation between the word or image that was quickly chosen or created for the purpose of that specific situation in time and place on the one hand, and the collection of possible words or experiences within an object, nation, animal or person, on the other. Only a very specific, temporary relation with a person or object's subcutaneous character exists. For the brain, the original meaning of words, characters and identities if they exist altogether, do not count, only their purpose in the new context.[38]

(36)
TRANSFORMER
'A Transformer is an intelligent machine that is able to "transform", reconfiguring itself into a common and innocuous form, such as a car, aircraft, or animal. The taglines "More Than Meets the Eye" and "Robots in Disguise" reflect this ability. Transformers originally featured two main factions warring for control of their home planet, Cybertron. The heroic Autobots (Cybertrons in the Japanese version) were led by Optimus Prime (known in the Japanese version as Convoy), and their opponents, the Decepticons (Destrons in the Japanese version), were led by Megatron.' -
http://en.wikipedia.org/wiki/Transformers Universes

(37)
APPROPRIATION
For many people the rise of the network society is closely related to the rise of the so-called capsular society. This is a society of gated communities, fear, exclusion and safety regulations. Real experiences are replaced by entertainment and spectacle, thus changing entire populations into 'hypnotized robots', 'living corpses' or 'dead wood floating down the river of time', to paraphrase some of the expressions used. The 'Society of the

Spectacle' is considered one of the main problems. Therefore, some of the theoreticians seem to suggest, shopping malls and entertainment centres should be dismantled and spectacular architecture should be forbidden. Which of course is a hell of a job because they are everywhere.
But there might be other solutions. In spite of the gated communities and the spectacles, there are always subtle and slow, underground changes that remain hidden before the eye. Shock wise changes in society may result from built-up underground tensions, like an earthquake that results from the tension between tectonic plates moving in different directions.
In theory, not every capsule is a disaster for the inhabitant or society. And not everything in the entertainment industry or the 'Society of the Spectacle' is harmful either. Many useful elements can be recycled and reprogrammed for future generations.
Each time we make new designs, we make changes to the way networks, capsules, spectacles and the everyday work in our society. Everything that is considered harmful for society at large or for me, can be appropriated and be made to function in a different way. Even when it is something many consider positive, whereas I don't. For example when it is society's taste for the total elimination of risk. We can even change taste. There

is no reason to get rid of things that we consider harmful, because, like the people before us, we can simply make them work differently. Dealing with the world of things is a constant dialogue with so-called autonomous processes and destiny.
Suggested reading:
Debord Guy (Society of the Spectacle); Darwin Charles (The Origin of Species); Nietzsche Friedrich (Happy Science); Dawkins Richard (The Selfish Gene)

(38)
BRAINS
New evidence and neurological theories seem to suggest that the brain does not choose from a catalogue of words and experiences that remains unchanged. Thinking, speaking and writing seem to be like building cars from a scrap heap. No element or combination of elements is used as their supposed 'original intention'. They are chosen for a new purpose and related to hitherto unknown experiences. To introduce a new metaphor, thinking and writing look a bit like scanning a waste disposal for useful material.

Identity and the essence of things, constantly escape our description and communication with people and objects that is based on image is tricky business.[39]

We are easily misled by skins, clothes, first impressions and old reputations. It does not really matter whether they are false or not because we cannot really tell the difference. That is why many of us rely on machines if they are shiny and produce a satisfying noise. If machines look good and we own them, we feel healthy ourselves. It is also why zebras in the wild are successful in escaping lions and why a butterfly has fake eyes on its wings. They purposely tell false stories – for example about their size – to a possible predator. Comparably, people use clothes to communicate their intentions and filmmakers, storytellers and journalists use images to work on the preconceptions that were created by our earlier experiences. Sometimes to adjust our ideas to their own experience of truth, which might indeed be necessary, but sometimes to deliberately misguide us or to create an exciting new perspective.

The message contained in the skin or clothes does not represent the identity of a person or object, nor does the skin of a building represent its interior. To be able to protect the indefinable and constantly changing interior of people and objects, and at the same time to attract others, clothes, cladding and skin should produce a seductive and repelling image simultaneously. This principle is often used by men and women who want to create an attractive image for others. The most attractive image is open to interpretation and change. It is a protective, aggressive, seductive and flexible communication tool with the environment.[40]

Skin and clothes have a long history, also in theories of art and architecture. The Dutch art historian Kees Vollemans for example, wrote a fascinating story about a painting of cows by the Dutch painter Henk Chabot. In his description it is a very ambiguous painting, as the viewer can see two things in the painting: a comforting landscape with cows or a shocking skin. At second glance a cow's head with an eye stares back at you stoically. By using the paint layer as a skin, the painting protects itself, as it were, confronting the viewer with his inquisitive gaze.[41]

(39)
EVOLUTION OF LANGUAGE AND ARCHITECTURE
In reproducing experiences, a culturally determined vocabulary is used. The personification of this reproduction is in the constellation and context of words: the sentence. Next the interpretation, an appropriation takes place, with the other causing a slight shift in meaning – in DNA terms a reproduction error. The quantity of suggestive gaps in communication determines the extent of appropriation and evolution. It does not matter if the interpretation is true or false, what counts is the applicability of an appropriation to new situations and demands. How does such an evolutionary process find a place in architectural design practice – a practice where dialogues with politicians, clients and users take place and where participants should be aware that a cultural message is disseminated?

Orders for designs result from the interaction between the traditional utilitarian demand and a very dynamic cultural context. Talking about architectural vocabulary is called typology. Types are not constant and cannot be collected in a toolbox, but are formulated according to topical needs and customs – types only exist in retrospect. By fitting in these newly discovered types in a new context, a change in meaning will take place time and again: a mutation takes place. The reference ensures a certain degree of communicability and practicability. The cohesion with other parts of the design in the new context is a sign of appropriation and adaptation to the example of changed circumstances.'
– Ton Venhoeven, Inaugural speech of 3 November 2006, University of Technology Eindhoven

(40)
THE PRINCIPLE OF CLADDING
Since the skin, or clothes, is everything we can possibly know, the architect Adolf Loos took the 'principle of cladding' as organising principle of his architecture. He 'borrowed' this principle from both Gottfried Semper, who related it to tent building in nomadic cultures, and Friedrich Nietzsche. Further down the road, Nietzsche's 'love for the surface' was probably appropriated from Darwin's The Origin of Species.

(41)
KEES VOLLEMANS
Vollemans Kees and Beks Maarten, Henk Chabot, concerterende landschappen, (concerting landscapes) (Zwolle: Waanders Publishers, 1989)

The skin of a building can also look back and protect the building and its residents against the curiosity of the outside world; the cladding conceals and may be seductive, but says little about the essence of the building, its interior. Or, as Adolf Loos indicated: the exterior is the reverse of the interior. Personal elements cannot be communicated with common words or images, they can, at most, be suggested 'between the lines'. The same is true for societies; appearances hide an underground with a lot of cultural contraband.

In cities, cultures, people and objects, there is always a tension between form and content or between skin and clothing. This tension can be related to the concept of 'suspense'.[42] By not yet completely specifying what something exactly is and by postponing actual meaning by means of deliberate incompleteness, a scenario writer can tease and torment the audience's longing for certainty. This principle of 'suspense' is used in film, literature and plays to evoke tension. This tension makes it possible for people to connect to the stars and it makes them wanting to know how the characters develop and the story unfolds.[43] The translation of suspense from film and theatre into architecture offers an escape to the constant pressure to produce buildings, cities (and countries) as illustration of a cultural identity. It also offers a lot of inspiration for the way in which you can tell your own fantastic stories.

(42)
SUSPENSE
'Suspense or tension is the feeling of uncertainty and interest about the outcome of certain actions an audience perceives in a dramatic work. According to Aristotle's Poetics, suspense is an important building block of drama. In very broad terms, it consists of having some real danger looming and a ray of hope. The two common outcomes can be: the danger hits, whereby the audience will feel sorrowful, or the hope comes true, whereby the audience will first feel joy, then satisfaction. If there is no hope, the audience will feel despair. – http://en.wikipedia.org/wiki/Suspense

(43)
PSYCHO
Psycho (1960) is a suspense/ thriller/horror film directed by world-renowned filmmaker Alfred Hitchcock. It is based on the novel by Robert Bloch, which was in turn based on the crimes of Wisconsin serial killer Ed Gein. The film depicts the encounter between a secretary who impulsively embezzles funds from her employer and a lonely, profoundly disturbed motel proprietor, Norman Bates. Psycho was the first film to introduce a single main character and then kill her halfway into the film with no apparent indication to the audience of how the story might progress after her death. That daring plot device, coupled with the fact that the character was played by the biggest box-office name in the film, was a shocking and disorienting turn of events in 1960. – http://en.wikipedia.org/wiki/Psycho %281960 film%29

E . V . E

05:00 am	Celebrities jogginghour
05:30 am	Early bird watching
06:30 am	Jogging for the millions
07:00 am	Tai Chi experience
08:00 am	Coffee with view over the Hudson
08:15 am	Walking the dog
08:30 am	Wake up snack on the way to the City
08:30 am	Outdoor aerobics on the lawn
08:45 am	Undress and put tie back on
09:00 am	Walking the baby
10:00 am	Fitness for hardbodies
10:15 am	Play soldier with daddy
10:45 am	Sit down for coffee
11:00 am	Join kids at kindergarden
11:05 am	Watching a game
12:00 am	Jumping on the aircushion
12:30 am	Lunch all over the place
01:00 pm	U-boat arrival
01:30 pm	Walking granny
02:00 pm	Baseballing, soccering, tennissing
02:00 pm	Volleyballing, basketballing, kayaking
02:30 pm	Picknick in the sun
02:45 pm	Helicopter sight seeing tour
03:00 pm	Hang around and do nothing
03:00 pm	Get laid in the grass
04:00 pm	Climbing the vulcano
04:00 pm	Buying a new skateboard
04:15 pm	Laptopping under the big oaktree
05:00 pm	Showtime
05:25 pm	Shopping on the way home
06.30 pm	Play squash
07:00 pm	Down town boys fitness
07:30 pm	Dinner at E.V.E
08:00 pm	Sunset in New Jersey
08:15 pm	Walking the dog again
08:45 pm	After dinner dip
09:00 pm	Art show vernissage
09:30 pm	Extraordinary vulcano experience
10:30 pm	Late barbecue party
11:00 pm	Stand-up comedian in the arena
11:15 pm	Moonlight romance
12:00 pm	Starlight rollerblading
00:15 am	Boat tour at night
00:30 am	Smashing Pumpkins on the lawn
01:00 am	Vulcanoclub junglesession
02:00 am	ABBA revival
03:00 am	Late night dance party
04:00 am	Fishing trout in the Hudson
04:15 am	After swing snack

EVE
New York, 1998

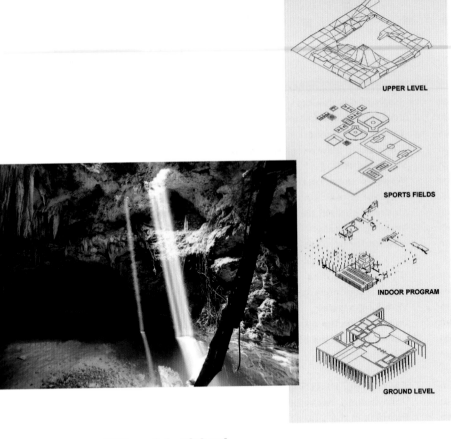

UPPER LEVEL

SPORTS FIELDS

INDOOR PROGRAM

GROUND LEVEL

EVE – a living island

In the autumn of 1998, we participated in an architectural competition concerning plans for a combination of a park and sports facility on the former pier of the Holland-America Line in Manhattan. After studying the programme of the sports complex, it turned out that it was not really possible to create the required park: the structure of the available space designated three quarters to sport and one quarter to park. Shortly before this, I had visited New York and noticed that the city seemed to be organized in an almost military fashion. Everything was linked to logistics, security, and the distinction between various functions, regardless of how close to one another they were. It seemed as if sport and fitness had been invented in New York as a kind of training programme to enable people to sustain life in the metropolis.

Taking this situation as the starting point, we formulated the idea that we could also create the park on top of the sports complex. We covered all the functions of the sports facility with park, with the exception of the pitches. The height differences could be used to generate an artificial hilly landscape, so that the park looked larger than it really was. It was as if a paradisiacal park was being used to camouflage the secret life in a criminal training camp. The combination of good and evil in the same object ensures subcutaneous tension and vagueness about the intentions of the project. Is this a critique of the city's contradictory culture or a nice place to walk the dog? At least it was an ideal combination for a recreation amenity.

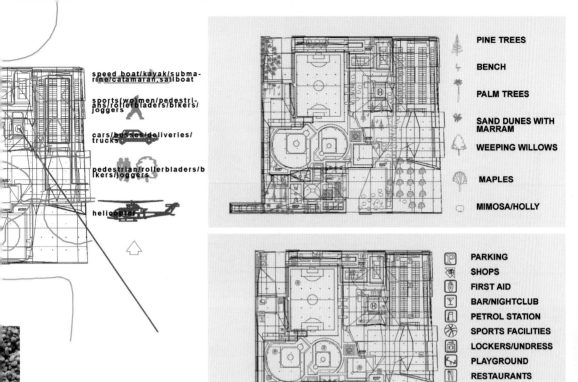

speed boat/kayak/subma-
rine/catamaran,sailboat

sports(women/pedestri-
ans/rollerbladers/bikers/
joggers

cars/busses/deliveries/
trucks

pedestrian/rollerbladers/b
ikers/joggers

helicopter

PINE TREES	
BENCH	
PALM TREES	
SAND DUNES WITH MARRAM	
WEEPING WILLOWS	
MAPLES	
MIMOSA/HOLLY	

P	PARKING
	SHOPS
	FIRST AID
Y	BAR/NIGHTCLUB
	PETROL STATION
	SPORTS FACILITIES
	LOCKERS/UNDRESS
	PLAYGROUND
	RESTAURANTS
	KIOSK
	RESTROOMS
	PICKNICK AREA

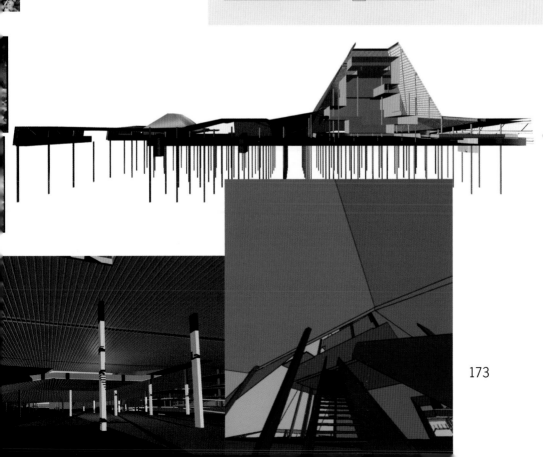

173

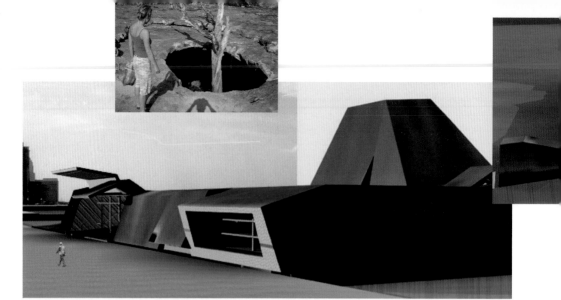

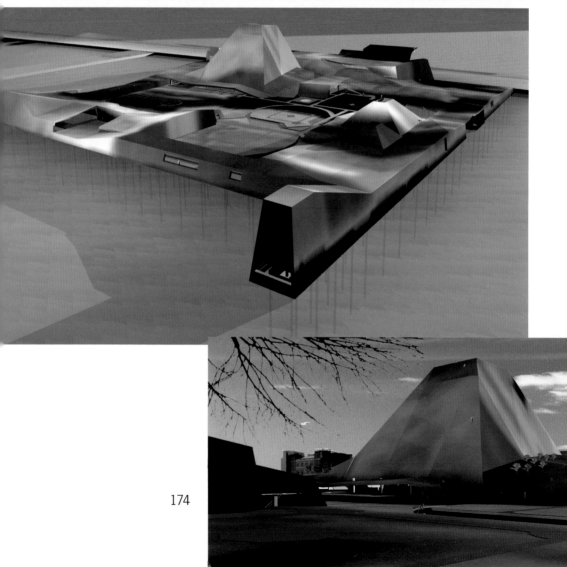

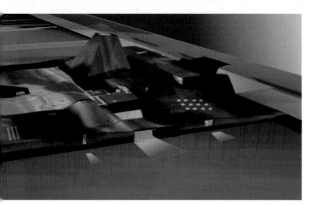

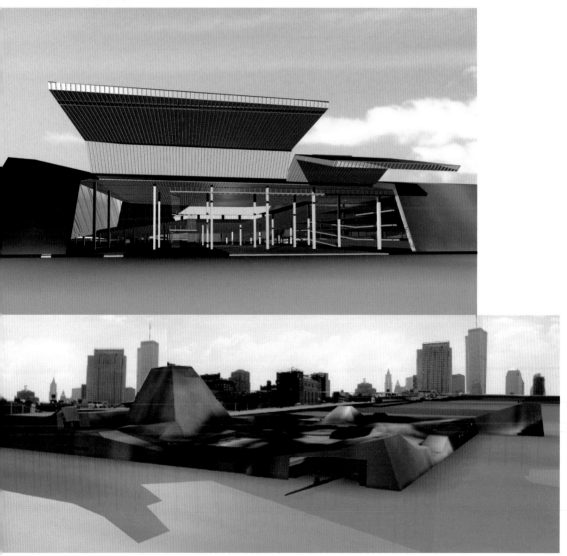

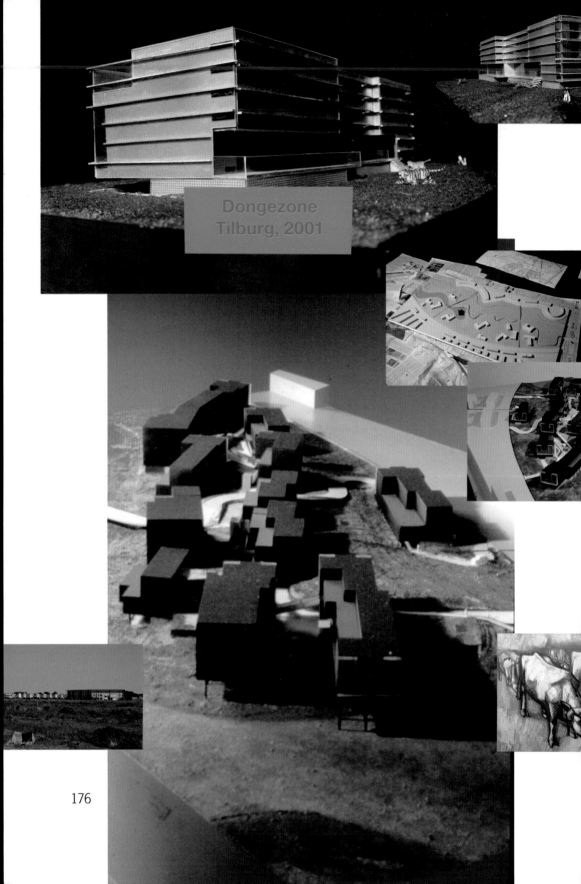

Dongezone
Tilburg, 2001

176

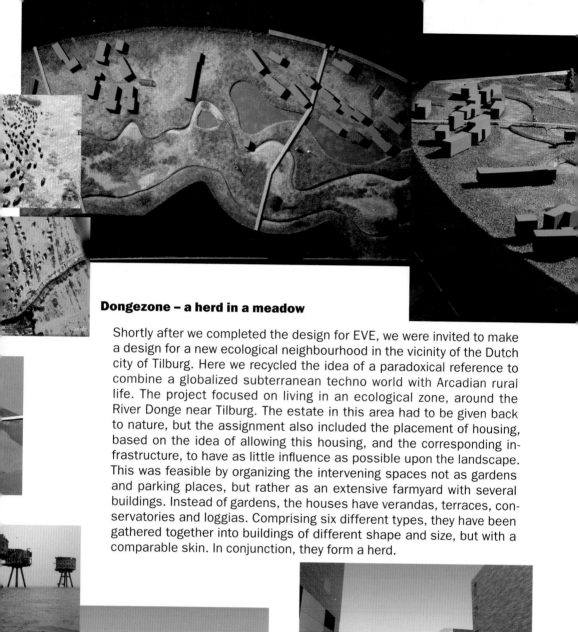

Dongezone – a herd in a meadow

Shortly after we completed the design for EVE, we were invited to make a design for a new ecological neighbourhood in the vicinity of the Dutch city of Tilburg. Here we recycled the idea of a paradoxical reference to combine a globalized subterranean techno world with Arcadian rural life. The project focused on living in an ecological zone, around the River Donge near Tilburg. The estate in this area had to be given back to nature, but the assignment also included the placement of housing, based on the idea of allowing this housing, and the corresponding infrastructure, to have as little influence as possible upon the landscape. This was feasible by organizing the intervening spaces not as gardens and parking places, but rather as an extensive farmyard with several buildings. Instead of gardens, the houses have verandas, terraces, conservatories and loggias. Comprising six different types, they have been gathered together into buildings of different shape and size, but with a comparable skin. In conjunction, they form a herd.

177

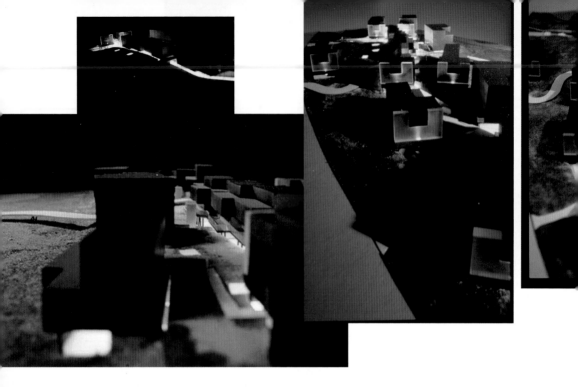

178

The context for this plan is a suburban environment, although the life-style does not differ much from that of the city. At first sight, it seems like an evocation of a small village with hammocks and free-range chickens. But there is a complex network of routes underground. Modern devices have been integrated into the buildings and they are equipped with all mod cons. There is tension between the local culture you see and this subcutaneous world that is linked to all kinds of worlds far beyond the village. The domain of cows and that of space travel are both present. It all depends on the way you look at it. During the daytime, the buildings stand peacefully amid the grass. But at night the light from the car parks makes them float like aliens.

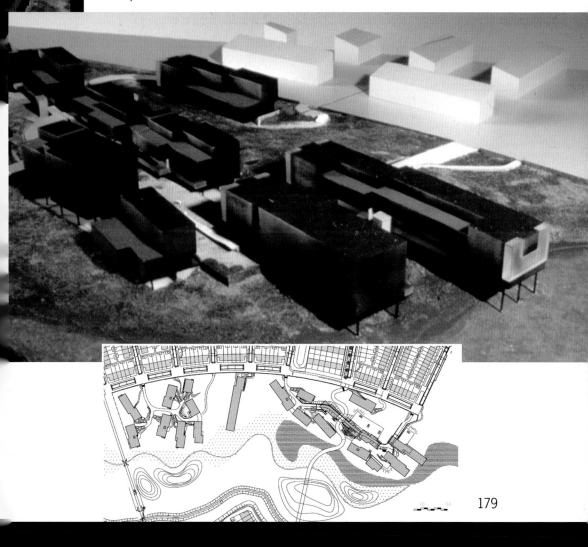

**Geinwijk, Bijlmermeer
Amsterdam, 1998**

Geinwijk – houses in urban bodies

Many buildings do have a life of their own and sometimes people even commit multiple murders on them. I became very aware of this when working on the Geinwijk project in the Bijlmermeer Amsterdam. The Bijlmermeer district has become a charged environment. If you work there, you are expected to participate in settling accounts with modernism and with the anonymity of modern life in apartment blocks. I did not share that a priori rejection of Modernism. In my opinion, buildings can change as people can. A dialogue with past ideologies is more interesting than an eradication followed by the construction of a new totalitarian ideology. It is much better to tackle pressing problems in the Bijlmer district by adding contemporary buildings and replacing only a few old and poor buildings with new construction. In doing so, you would renew the fabric of the neighbourhood, revive its potential and enrich it with an extra, historical layer at the same time. In spite of this, I accepted the assignment to make a plan for single-family homes with gardens to replace the demolished high-rise apartments in Geinwijk.

Participating in this kind of assignment means that you cannot avoid taking a critical approach to your own attitude on the assignment and on politics in general. The flexibility and modernity of the lively, informal atmosphere of the old, multicultural Bijlmer district had to be replaced by a new ideology – that of suburban single-family suburban homes with a clear identity and a strict distinction between public and private.

To make sure that a form of urbanity would arise and that all different kinds of people would be able to find a niche in the new Bijlmer, we developed buildings in which as many residential typologies as possible, and different sorts of occupants and lifestyles, could find a place. Further, by making flexible floor plans, each individual home could be inhabited in all kinds of different ways.

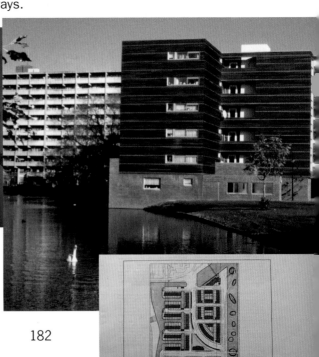

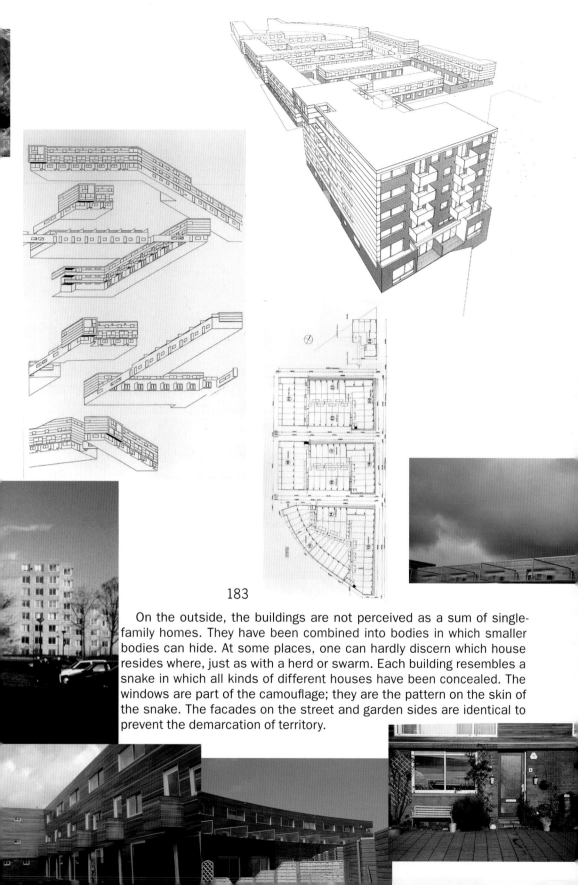

183

On the outside, the buildings are not perceived as a sum of single-family homes. They have been combined into bodies in which smaller bodies can hide. At some places, one can hardly discern which house resides where, just as with a herd or swarm. Each building resembles a snake in which all kinds of different houses have been concealed. The windows are part of the camouflage; they are the pattern on the skin of the snake. The facades on the street and garden sides are identical to prevent the demarcation of territory.

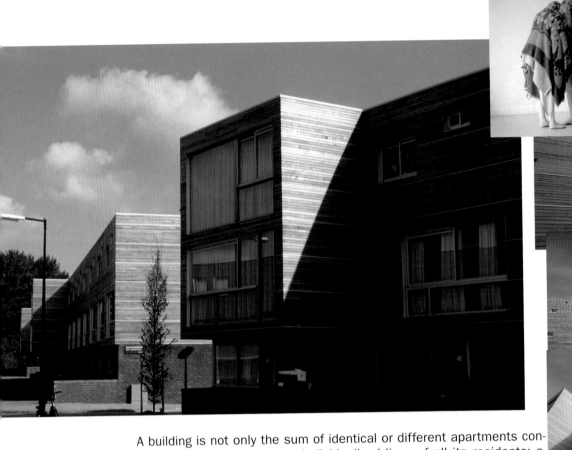

A building is not only the sum of identical or different apartments containing the standardized or individualized lives of all its residents; a building must also be able to lead its own life. Even though a building seems to be some sort of unit on the outside, you will be able to find an enormous assembly of differing things on the inside. Comfort and discomfort exist side by side in buildings because humans determine not everything.

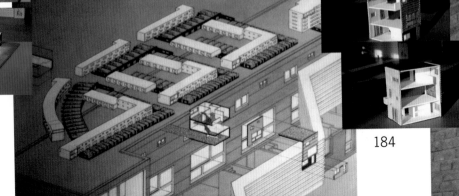

184

In several of our projects you can observe how an architectural body can consist of a collection of various components and ambiences, all of which reflect the animistic life of objects and their particular qualities. This animistic culture goes back to pre monotheistic times and can still be recognized in many contemporary religions and cultures. The notion that things lead their own lives, and are entitled to do so, is a reaction to the age-old idea that humans should control their destiny. In modern times this imperative was developed into the idea that this should be done by means of instruments. Even people themselves were supposed to become instruments to adapt themselves to a mechanistic interpretation of the cosmos. Globalization confronted this mainly Western concept with other cultural perspectives on our environment and due to global warming and other environmental disasters, the idea has become totally obsolete.

An animistic vision is already visible in music, poetry and the visual arts to a much greater extent than in architecture. It's not that architects and clients have nothing to do with this theme; it is rather a lack of awareness of other than human factors determining architectural results. It is not always 'we' who really want things, often the culture we live in wants us to want things. There are creatures other than people with a say in design matters, things and words want certain things. This animistic vision results in an everyday culture that is not based on the presumption that people and objects are mere instruments. It is based on the idea that people and things are in constant dialogue.

185

186

Rietlanden
Amsterdam, 2001

189

193

Rietlanden – a metal jacket

The location of the Rietlanden did not at all resemble the one in Gein-wijk. Therefore, the resulting designs are totally different, even though they were designed simultaneously. Here, the project involved the East-ern Docklands in Amsterdam, with a view of the busiest traffic hub in the city. The architecture had to enter into a dialogue with this mobility. According to the urbanistic requirements, the facades had to be made of aluminium in contrast with the surrounding brick buildings. The inten-tion was not to embed the envisaged five medium-rise buildings in the ground, but rather to 'park' them on the site, like trucks parked amid the scenery. This should prevent the privatization of the area because it was destined to become a public park. As a result, the architecture would acquire the form of a piece of equipment (a fridge, computer or stereo set). So instead of creating buildings rooted in the ground, we manufactured a set of robots with their own lives and their own counte-nances.

194

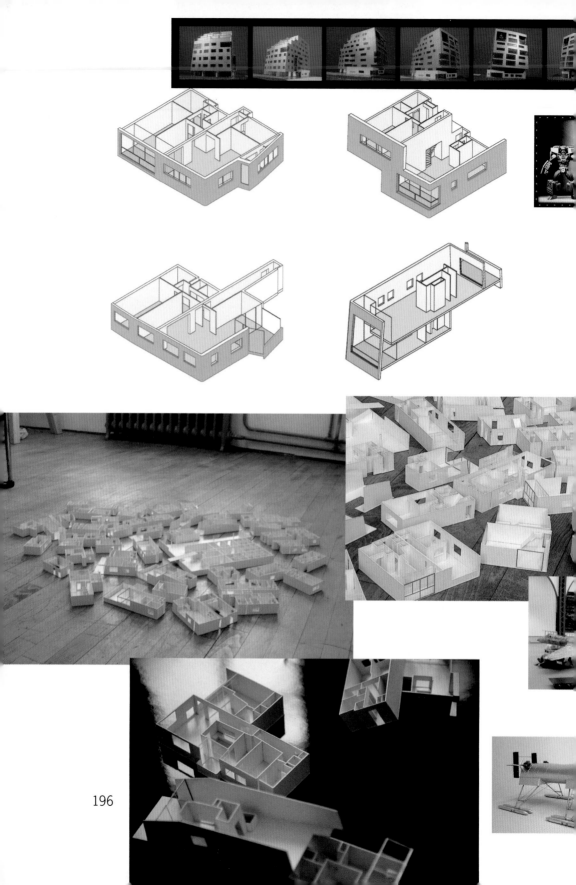

196

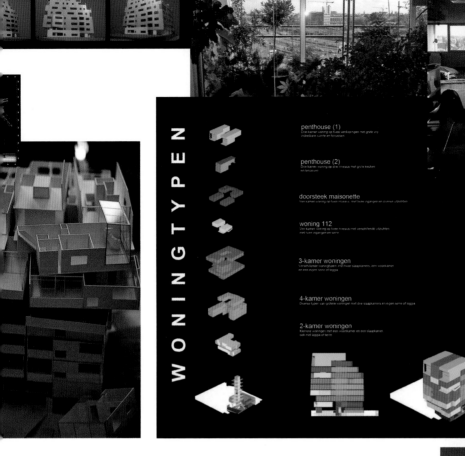

To respect and reflect the multitude of things (houses, windows, ideas) in the buildings, the houses and windows were allowed to express themselves by choosing their own preferred arrangement, shape and position. Further, we wanted the skin of the buildings to possess a kind of vulnerability or softness like what you occasionally see in art: as in the small melancholy lead aeroplanes by Anselm Kiefer, for example, or the felt objects produced by Joseph Beuys.[44,45] To realize this, the Rietlanden project made use of an aluminium plate cassette, which was thinner than the standard cassette, so that it would already look bumpy during construction. It was a cassette that would grow old gracefully. The pattern of the cladding does not faithfully follow the shape of the building. Just as with the clothes of many fashion designers, the cut does not automatically follow the line of the body, there is always intervening space.

(44)
ANSELM KIEFER

Anselm Kiefer's Melancholia 1990-91) is one of four large-scale ead sculpture airplanes that the artist created in the past decade. In both its title and its form, Melancholia makes reference to Albrecht Dürer's Melencolia I from 1514, which epresents the melancholic temperament through a depiction of an angel-winged woman sitting grounded with her head in her hands, a tetrahedron ositioned on the left side of the work.

Kiefer's lead-winged creation with a crystal tetrahedron on its left side recalls the ravages of the air raids of World War II, which ended the year the artist was born. Kiefer's art explores recent German history without memorializing; rather, it speaks of a transcendence of such oppositions as spiritual and material, heaven and earth, emphasized through his use of ed airplane. Kiefer chooses his mate-rial, in this case lead, not only for its physical properties, but for its signify-

ing values as well. Kiefer's sculptures in lead comment on the dual nature of ideas, history and forms of expression, exposing what is 'real' by encompassing oppositions. – Gerardo Herreros, www.herreros.com.ar/melanco/kiefer.htm

(45)
JOSEPH BEUYS

Joseph Beuys, the artist who was many times depicted by Andy Warhol actually became famous by his Aktionen (action events). He was a

member of the Fluxus movement and founder of the Green party in Germany, probably his most important Aktion (action and event). He used his memory of the Second World War in many of his works. Felt and fat helped him as a victim who survived an air crash, and they were used in many melancholical works. Like when he used a grand piano without legs and clad it with felt. You do not know whether to feel sorry for Beuys or for the piano. Check the Internet for Joseph Beuys!

198

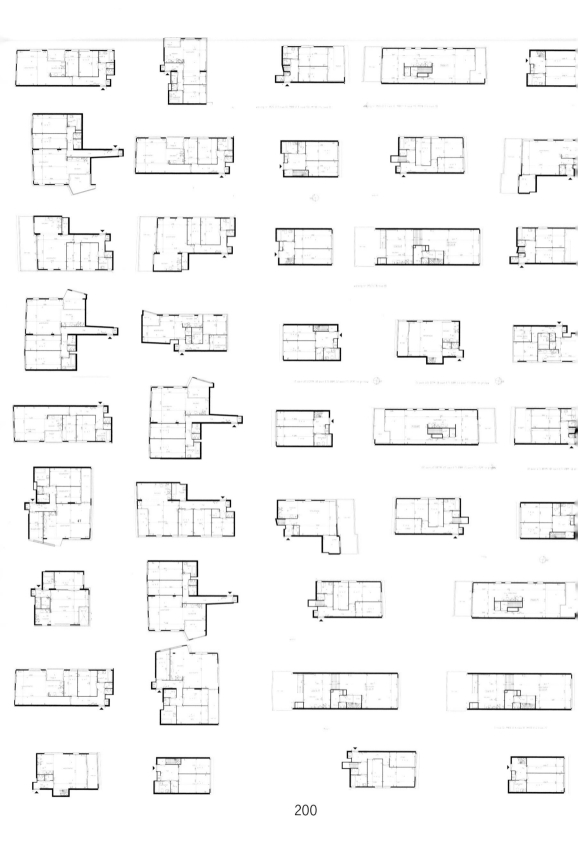

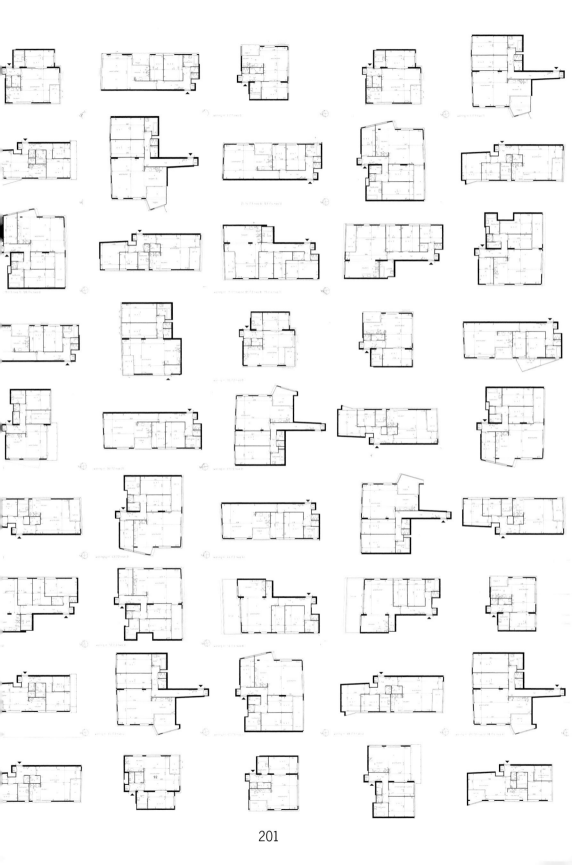

201

U2 Geuzenveld
Amsterdam, 2001

203

U2 Geuzenveld – bodywork of a hybrid building

When working on U2 Geuzenveld in 1997, we were confronted with yet another situation. We had to build this project amidst a famous town plan of Van Eesteren, a socialist garden city and city extension plan from the thirties in the western part of Amsterdam. This neighbourhood had deteriorated by conflicts between the older autochthonous population and recent immigrants attracted by cheap housing. On different sides of the project one could find low-rise and medium rise buildings from the modern era, some of which were in a good shape, others soon to be demolished. In the long run, the whole area was to transform into a denser urban environment. Here we had to respect the surrounding buildings and try to fit in with a high-density project. In contrast with the mono functional housing blocks, our project contained a range of different apartments, houses, shops and homes for elderly psychiatric patients.

The shape of the building was the result of negotiations with neighbourhood representatives (who didn't want extra houses because they might block the sun and claim extra parking places), politicians (who wanted city renewal, a mixed population and extra houses and shops) and our client, a housing corporation (who wanted to improve the neighbourhood with new and improved houses). We took these requirements as a natural start of our project and made a combination of classical modern design principles and contemporary demands. Respecting existing local traditions the building uses hygienistic design rules of transparency and outdoor living. Apart from its strange geometry, looked at from the outside, this building looks simply like a contemporary version of the modern principles. You see a lot of glass and a lot of repetition. This exterior plays a social role. Neighbours require respect and good behaviour from the new building.

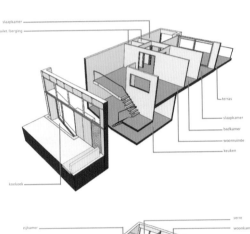

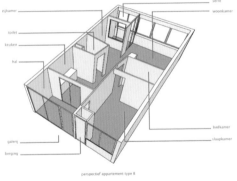

perspectief appartement type 8

206

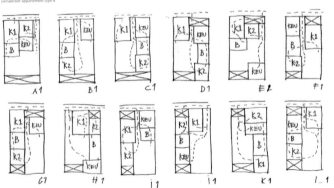

| ROUTES DOOR DE WONING. | BEUKMAAT HOH 7.2 M DIEPTE WONING 12.0 M | K 1 = GROTE SLAAPKAMER K 2 = KLEINE " B = BAD + BERGING | KEU = KEUK ⊠= BUIT |

But the skin of U2 Geuzenveld plays a double role: it communicates with the outside world and protects the interiors. Below the flexible glass surface, it hides many different functions and many different apartments. The skin makes only marginal distinction between open and closed parts. Glass extends everywhere – as clothing with a woven pattern – and has been applied not only for its transparency but also because of its reflective and translucent character. In this skin, everything is concealed.

207

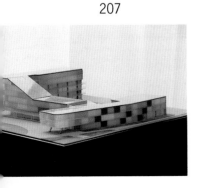

The houses in this project have conservatories that can be used as interior or exterior spaces. As a consequence of the manner in which the spaces have been grouped within the houses, they can be used in various ways. Thus, each resident can create a unique home. The interior is the place of personal experience. It is complex and allows leeway for all the contradictions and alterations inherent in life. So the interior accepts all good and bad tastes of the residents. These differences radiate through the skin of the building, which in itself tells a story about metamorphosis: how buildings and people consistently allow various accumulations of characters and qualities to flow effortlessly into one another.

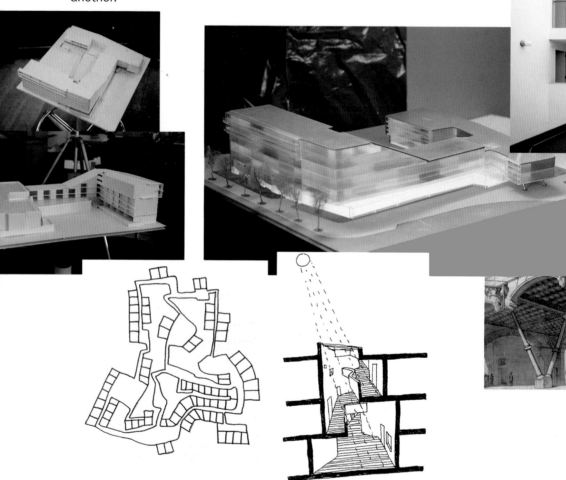

Besides various types of houses and apartments, this building also contains shops and a psychiatric residential amenity. This part of the building is intended for elderly people suffering from manic depression and schizophrenia, and for patients with Korsakov's syndrome, with a very limited short-term memory. The experiential world of these patients has become extremely small and, accordingly, this residential amenity is designed as a world in itself. Voids in a kind of 'Village Street' ensure the incidence of light between the houses. The surgeries of the doctors, the working areas, and the living rooms have been distributed along this street so that patients are stimulated to take a walk when they commute 'from their homes to work'. At the end of their street they have a super-conservatory, a kind of village pub with a view of the other world. It is a village in a building in the city.

SUPER
SERRE

288 t/m 310

286

U3 Geuzenveld
Amsterdam, 2006

215

216

U3 Geuzenveld (De Drie Bouwmeesters) – a village under a rock

In other projects, too, we work with the combination of an artificial skin and the fractal principle of a town in a building in a city. One of the examples can be found in the buildings adjoining U2, the U3 housing project. The lower floors of these buildings are designed to resemble houses hewn out of the foot of a steep mountain slope, so the upper parts of the buildings are made as abstract, solid blocks, reflecting the sky. To create the impression of solid rock, stucco plaster is applied everywhere. Miniature buildings are built in the various gateways.

217

Every individual house is structured like a small village square with the rooms functioning like surrounding houses. There are no corridors. These buildings are not only inhabited by people, pets and other animals, but also by buildings, cities and villages.

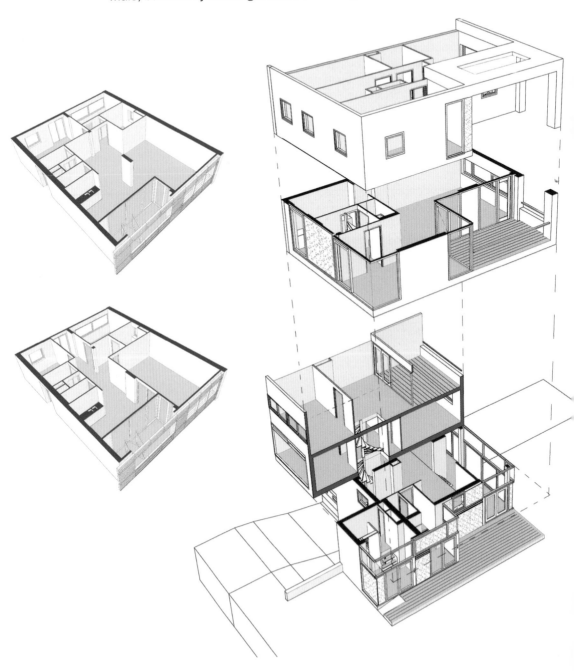

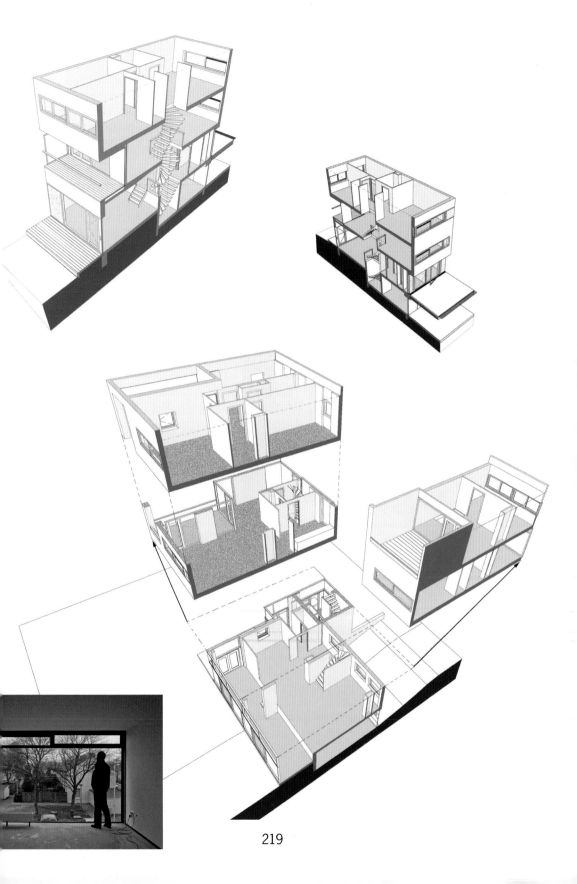

219

221

Blasio Inflatable Bouncer
Rotterdam, 1998

Blasio – space mountain

Living with people, animals and things is often a challenge for every-one's communication skills. Luckily playing and dancing are also part of social life.

To mark the occasion of its tenth anniversary the Netherlands Archi-tecture Institute's former director Kristin Feireiss organized a multiple assignment for an inflatable bouncer, in cooperation with the Rotter-dam Blasio Foundation. The design was realized by former drug addicts under the supervision of the Blasio Foundation and was initiated by ten-year-old children. The Blasio Foundation has made our inflatable bouncer available for rent for some years.

224

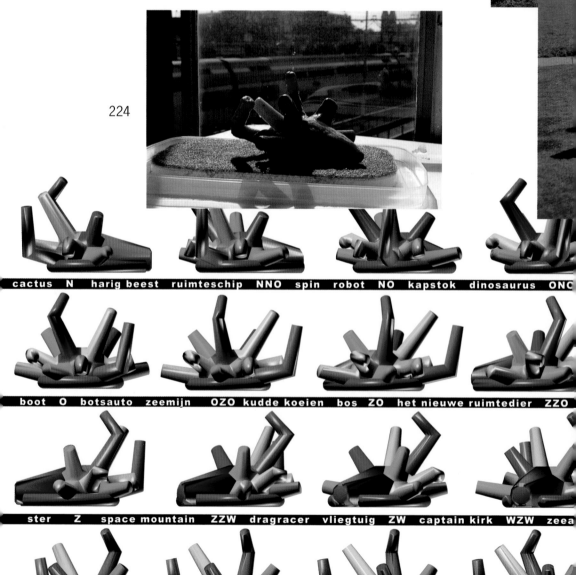

cactus N harig beest ruimteschip NNO spin robot NO kapstok dinosaurus ONO

boot O botsauto zeemijn OZO kudde koeien bos ZO het nieuwe ruimtedier ZZO

ster Z space mountain ZZW dragracer vliegtuig ZW captain kirk WZW zeea

The design consists of a colourful bouncer measuring 6 x 6 x 4 metres, in the form of (according to interpretation): a sweet monster, ship, forest, insect, hairy animal, sea anemone, star, joker, animal, mountain, cactus, flower, space animal, alien, space mountain, dodgem car, aeroplane, drag-racer, captain kirk, dinosaur, spider, lion, sea mine, herd of cows, porcupine, robot, coat stand, boat, tree, ashtray, and a spilled bag of French fries. The spiky form was produced by welding cylinder-shaped tubes to a hemisphere, with pentagons connected to hexagons. The complex form of the bouncer offers a great diversity of play possibilities, such as jumping, sliding, wrestling, hanging and climbing.

225

Abrixas – passion of a satellite

Often a skin is not a physical thing but rather an image, or an illusion that plays tricks on us. As a result, relations between people and things can develop in many strange directions. Especially in love affairs, mis-understandings can create numerous tragedies as appears from this contemporary opera. We took part in the development of its animistic concept and we designed the stage set.

How come it is so hard to know each other like in the triangular rela-tionship that is the subject of this opera? Sure, it is hard for a singer to understand the emotions and the technological complexity of a satellite, as it is hard for a scientist to understand a beautiful singer. And how about the pitiful satellite, who cannot reach the scientist, nor respond to the advances made by the singer?

People and things are too complex to even understand themselves, let alone others. People, things and buildings are like separate commu-nities, assembled from comparably complex parts. It is hard to speak of a knowable identity that we can really communicate with. We only have our image of others to rely on.[46]

---

(46)
ABRIXAS

A scientist who falls in love with a sing-er. A singer who asks for enlighten-ment from a satellite. A satellite that writhes free of the grasp of its crea-tor, the scientist, and captures the heart of the singer. This is the true-life story of ABRIXAS, the German sat-ellite that was intended to measure the entire heavens, right down to the background noise of the Big Bang, but severed contact with its base and only wished to communicate with the singer. A triangular relationship arises. The scientist writes letters to the singer about the launch and loss of ABRIXAS. He hardly knows her, but once heard her sing Erwartung by Schönberg. The scientist wishes to get through to her with his report about the satellite, just like ABRIXAS is destined to penetrate the depths of the universe, the only area that is still pristine and is yet to be conquered and developed by mankind. When the woman, confused by the letters, turns to the heavens, ABRIXAS applies its all-hearing capacity to win her heart. The makers present the tragicomical essence of mankind. In its yearning for union with the opposite sex, and in its foolish but irresistible passion to

know its place in the cosmos and the origins of its existence, humankind is just like the satellite ABRIXAS: a body floating helplessly in space, vainly seeking contact.

ABRIXAS :...
Singer : Hello... hello... ABRIXAS!

(3) Sung
Is everything gone? Is everything lost?

If only you were here. Your voice a silver light, your voice the wind that moves the branches.

You are bathed in light. Your eyes blue... deep-blue, like the evening twilight.

Where did I see you? In Munich? Karlsruhe? When?

He contacted us. He did what we asked, he turned to the sun. But the main battery became too hot, a wire loosened, the voltage diminished and since then poor ABRIXAS has been trying to straighten up only to fall back again. A spasm, every ninety seconds.

Spoken
Singer : ...
Singer : Come on, pick it up ...
Singer : ...
Singer : Ach, ach...

Singer : ...
Singer : Ach, ach, ABRIXAS...
Singer : ....
Singer : Are you ignoring me too?
Singer : ...

Edzard Mik, excerpt from Abrixas (libretto)

'Die wissenschaftliche Mission von ABRIXAS ist gescheitert.

Am 1. Juli 1999 hat das Deutsche Zentrum für Luft- und Raumfahrt (DLR) die wissenschaftliche Mission des Röntgensatelliten ABRIXAS offiziell für gescheitert erklärt. Bereits kurz nach dem Start am 28. April 1999 war die Hauptbatterie des Kleinsatelliten durch Überhitzung ausgefallen und wenige Tage später der Kontakt zum Satelliten abgerissen.

Der Fehlschlag von ABRIXAS ist wis-senschaftlich ein herber Verlust, nicht nur für die drei beteiligten deutschen Institute -- das Astrophysikalisches In-stitut Potsdam (AIP), das Max-Planck-Institut für extraterrestrische Physik (MPE) und das Institut für Astron-omie und Astrophysik der Universität Tübingen (IAAT); die Pfadfinderrolle von ABRIXAS durch die vollständige Durchmusterung des Himmels im

mittelenergetischen Röntgenbereich war bereits international fest einge plant und als Voraussetzung für weiter reichende Projekte betrachtet worden.

Original press release of MPE and AIP of 12 July 1999 after losing contact with the satellite. Check the Internet for Abrixas!

226

227

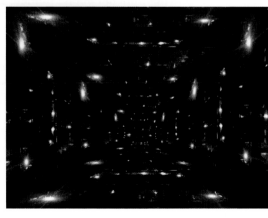

Microcosms (47,48)

For all the persons on board of Noah's Ark it was not only impossible to leave their floating world – there was no need either. After all, their entire world was incorporated in the ark.[49] Spaceships for intergalactic journeys that take thousands of years, also possess this property: in order to offer the people and animals on board a life similar to that on earth during their spaceflights, they must be designed as completely autarkic worlds. We come across all aspects of life on board, varying from networks, fabrics, bodies, herds and skins, to life, reproduction and death.

(47)
GO
'The Ancient Japanese considered the Go board to be a microcosm of the universe. Although when it is empty it appears to be simple and ordered, in fact, the possibilities of gameplay are endless. They say that no two Go games have ever been alike. Just like snowflakes. So, the Go board actually represents an extremely complex and chaotic universe.' – Sol Robeson in the movie Pi, www.pithemovie.com/go.html

(48)
FRACTAL
'In colloquial usage, a fractal is a shape that is recursively constructed or self-similar, that is, a shape that appears similar at all scales of magnification and is therefore often referred to as "infinitely complex". Mathematicians avoid giving the strict definition and prefer to regard a fractal as a geometric object that has most or all of the following features, it: has fine structure at arbitrarily small scales; is too irregular to be easily described in traditional Euclidean geometric language; is self-similar (at least approximately or stochastically); has a Hausdorff dimension greater than its topological dimension; and has a simple and recursive definition.

Not all self-similar objects are fractals – for example, the real line (a straight Euclidean line) is formally self-similar but fails to have other fractal characteristics. The term fractal was coined in 1975 by Benoît Mandelbrot, from the Latin fractus meaning "broken" or "fractured".' http://en.wikipedia.org/wiki/Fractal

(49)
NOAH'S ARK
Noah was a mythical figure described in the Bible. He built a ship to save the world, after God warned him that a big flood would come to punish mankind. Check the Bible for Noah's Ark!

228

A manifestation like this does not imply that the ark or the space-craft contains a capsular society **in extremis**, but conversely offers an alternative for hyper-comfort and isolation inside the usual capsules. The notion of 'exclusion' from the world outside the capsule is replaced by the notion of inclusion in the unusual object of the world's complexity. Thus the object becomes a microcosm in which all aspects of life are represented. Buildings designed according to this principle might be called laboratories of life. They are present in the world as heterotopias, but contain complete parallel worlds as well.

Interaction between the inside and the outside world takes place at specific moments and in strategic places. The breathing skin is thus given a hybrid function: on the one hand it excludes the outside world, on the other it keeps the inside world together and nurtures it with fresh air, food, vitamins and sensual encounters with the outside world. The skin of a building is an interface. Not only the safe everyday things of life are admitted in the interior, but occasionally also the adventurous unknown things. This microcosm is not a gated community, but a living body.

The combination of people, animals, things and illusions within an object or person is a sublime, fractal landscape with steep canyons and vertiginous abysses, or, maybe a more suitable description, a giant Network City. <u>S t a r w a r s</u> 'Death star' is a good image for this.[50] Cities are networks and constellations of biological, cultural, social and psychological connections, they are a bit like the brains of a person or animal, or to put it bluntly, they are microcosms.

(50)
DEATH STAR
he Death Star was an enormous
iilitary battle station in the fictional
tar Wars universe. Two of them
vere built over the course of the sees (although the real model, about 2
/2 feet in diameter, currently resides
n Seattle's Pacific Science Center);

they are enormous space stations
capable of destroying a planet completely.' Check the Internet!

In 1969, the late Buckminster Fuller designed a dome encasing midtown Manhattan, thus turning an entire city into a giant climatized building, or a brainpan.[51] If his design would have been executed, all formerly freestanding buildings would suddenly share the same interior space. I admire the futuristic aspects of this proposal and maybe the idea could be developed further to save energy in existing cities. Apart from that, and maybe more important, it is a seductive proposal to merge the definitions of building and city into a microcosm.[52]

History shows numerous examples where the merging of city and building was achieved before. Palaces such as the 'Forbidden City' in Beijing were designed as cities. Fortresses, Imperial Roman baths, churches and also medieval walled cities were designed or looked like buildings containing cities. Many cities all over the world were designed as houses in which the inhabitants shared the same interior space. But maybe the strongest examples of interior public spaces are to be found in subterranean cities.

Everywhere in the world, from Petra in Jordan to the Allora caves in India and Mesa Verde in Colorado, people made subterranean houses, graveyards, churches and temples, sometimes in combination with artificial structures, roughly comparable to the way termites build termite hills in the landscape. There, from the outside, you hardly see anything, maybe a small hilly structure, but when looking inside, you see an almost infinite, organically grown world, a city in itself. For people and animals it is a safe way to defend the community against everyday perils. Even now, people build underground bunkers with all kinds of secret spaces, sometimes equipped with the most extravagant luxury and technological appliances. Some of those resemble entire cities hidden from view.

(51)
BUCKMINSTER FULLER
Buckminster Fuller found language to be the first industrial tool. To describe the complex system of planet earth, he invented new words and word combinations such as omni-interac-commodative. The word 'Universe' to him meant 'the sum of all experience'. Buckminster Fuller, was very strongly interested in the future of our planet. According to him, the world should be looked upon as a system that needed maintenance. In his book O p e r a t- i n g M a n u a l f o r S p a c e s h i p E a r t h, he related earth to a spaceship flying through space. The spaceship has a finite amount of resources and cannot be resuppplied. Fuller Buckminster, O p e r a t i n g M a n u a l f o r S p a c e s h i p E a r t h (1963)

(52)
MICROCOSM
Buckminster Fuller's definition of 'Universe' as 'the sum of all experience' is also used in the designs of VenhoevenCS. In daily life, the word microcosm is used to describe a complex constellation of objects, words and people that can hardly be described otherwise. In the tradition of architectural design practice and theory however, a building can be seen as a microcosm referring to, and explaining the 'Divine Principles' of the greater cosmos. We, at VenhoevenCS,

do not speak about 'Divine Principles of the Universe', but prefer to use the more common meaning and build real microcosms of the 'Universe' instead. We make cosmopolitan capsules, artificial spaces that contain 'the sum of all experience', constellations of objects, things, words and people, not the 'divine' principles.

The microcosm of the building,' or city configuration, is traditionally a pars pro toto of the universe. This tradition, to make buildings and cities as microcosms, goes back to ancient times when, for example, the Egyptians positioned the centre of the pyramid constellation, Giza along the river Nile to reflect the Milky Way and Orion. In many old cultures such examples can be found and they were often used to reinforce the existing organization of society. Aesthetic rules of the composition of an architectural body followed the supposed (or desired) rules of the universe. Within the composition, as within society, the rules were used to identify 'others', threats to unity and harmony. Such 'Others', elements that were considered being a threat to the 'natural order' were expelled, or removed from the composition. Over the ages however, many composition rules have been developed according to false interpretations of so-called 'universal laws' and many of such rules still survive in contemporary architectural

practice, with undesired effects. In the old days, the supposed hierarchical organization of the universe inspired architects and politicians to reflect this idea in the absolute organization of the palace at Versailles. Another conception, the eighteenth century idea of the cosmos as a giant clockwork, derived from Newton's 'Principia', still operates in today's conception of buildings as functional utensils with predictable effects, and in the nineteenth century, the encyclopedia of Linnaeus led architects to believe that building types should be regarded as distinct and unchangeable, an idea we still find in many generic building types and components. One might say the encyclopedia has developed into the moral imperative of 'shopping'. Unconsciously we tend to see buildings arranged according to such principles as beautiful configurations, but they are also confirmations of the way we think about the world.

From a theoretical perspective, they can be seen as microcosms with moral power, because the idea that the composition rules reflect cosmic principles, gives them unchallenged, theological authority. Since many aesthetic principles are closely related to long-gone and current misinterpretations of the universe, and since their effect on the contemporary world is sometimes pretty detrimental, challenging and redefining the cosmic

principles underlying contemporar architecture is the least we can do.
This challenging applies to the functionalistic and generic everyda buildings and cities as well as to th current hype of blob architecture. Th latter one is a contemporary example of a misinterpretation of the univers Overestimated 'blob' architecture, to gether with all the meanings surroun ing it, has a strong potential for be coming the next moral and cultural in perative, because it is closely linke to worn-out ideals of liberalism an globalization. We currently witnes that the suggested free flow of info mation, people, and organizations re sults in the rise of a fear society figh ing terrorism wherever the free flo is prohibited. In spite of the utopia expectations of its protagonists, blo architecture is an advertising for th free flow of capital and the principle c exclusion of anything other than th global, the flexible and the generic.

Suggested reading:
Prigogine, Ilya and Isabell Stengers, O r d e r o u t o f C h a o s M a n ' s n e w d i a l o g u e w i t n a t u r e (Toronto, New York, Londo Sydney: 1984); Hardt, Michael an Negri Antonio, E m p i r e (Cambridg MA: Harvard University Press, 2000)

Subterranean cities present the most extreme examples of an effect that can be witnessed also in stand-alone buildings: on the outside, such buildings look much smaller than the space you experience on the inside. The inside of those buildings contain, seemingly autonomous worlds, or, one might say, autonomous cities. Just like the concept of a 'city as a house', the 'city in a building' is an age-old design principle that can be found in all kinds of buildings all over the world. In the old days, an architect would repeat, show or hide elements that looked like autonomous buildings in different scales in the interior or exterior of a building. Often these elements were used to create spatial experiences interwoven with cultural and political meanings, statements and narratives.

In the twentieth century, the philosopher Michel Foucault, the cultural theorist Walter Benjamin and the architectural theorist Beatriz Colomina, all wrote about this design principle and its application in contemporary architecture.[53,54] In the interior and the skin of a house, an architect can express his ideas on society and the cosmos. The architect Adolf Loos was just one of the many famous architects who used the idea of microcosms and society in the Raumplan design of his houses.[55] The outside of his famous Villa Müller for example, is of little interest. The skin of the building is neutrally clad with white stucco, like a gentleman's white smoking. In this way, the building participates in the urban landscape as a physical body, in a seductive, but almost polite way. What a difference with the inside! Here, all great cultures of the world can be discovered in an exciting constellation of high and low, real and virtual spaces, folded and wrapped around winding routes and secret places. Beyond the threshold, this building is infinitely bigger than its appearance on the outside. That is no building, it is a person!

(53)
WALTER BENJAMIN
enjamin Walter, Berlin Childood around 1900 (Cambridge, MA: Harvard University Press, 2006)

(54)
BEATRIZ COLOMINA
olomina, Beatriz, Privacy and ublicity: Modern Architecture as Mass Media (Cambridge, MA: MIT Press, 1996)

(55)
VILLA MÜLLER
ne of the last works of Adolf Loos, is famous Villa Müller is a good example of the Raumplan principle e applied to organizing space. In Raumplan cubic spaces at different levels are wrapped around an mpty' central space. Each space is ad with different materials and colurs such as travertine marble, green enamel, white gypsum, dark brown wood and many others. These claddings often refer to separate world cultures. From every individual space it is possible to watch people moving through other spaces. The route through the house is a staging of different cultural experiences through a miniature world.

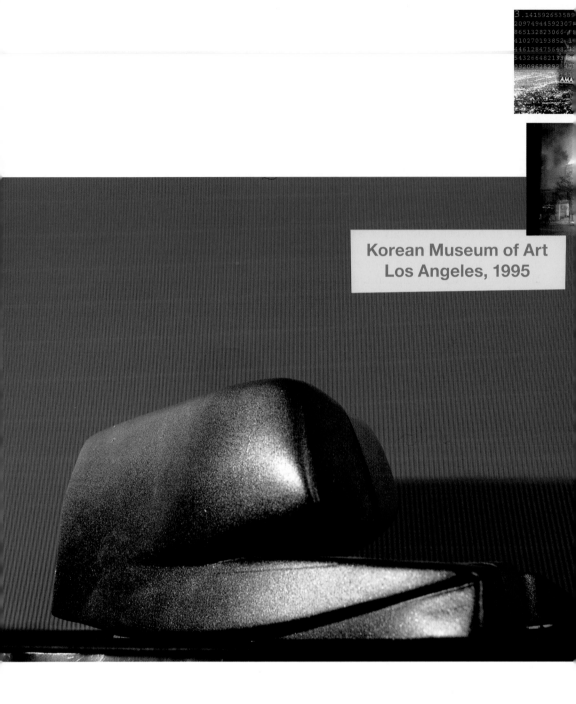

Korean Museum of Art
Los Angeles, 1995

KOMA – the world inside a public image

When I was in Los Angeles in 1994, the city had just had this earthquake and shortly before there had been massive racial riots. Korean shopkeepers in particular had fallen victim to these disturbances. They were recent immigrants and successful into the bargain; they were reputed to snap up all the good jobs. Because they formed a closed community, they were willing victims of xenophobia. After that frightful event, the Korean community wanted to restore their image, so it organized a competition for a Korean cultural centre and museum of Korean culture. We took part in that competition with a design that combines a multitude of elements from Korean history.

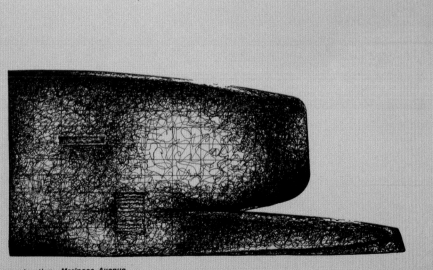

elevation Mariposa Avenue

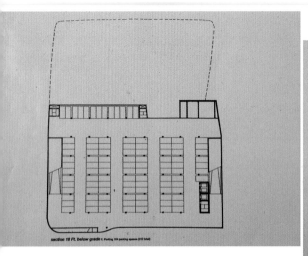

section 18 Ft. below grade 1: Parking 104 parking spaces (312 total)

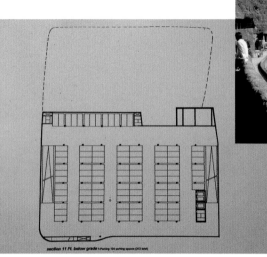

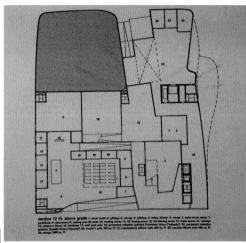

section 11 Ft. below grade 1: Parking 104 parking spaces (312 total)

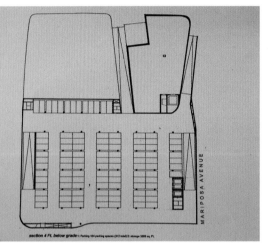

section 4 Ft. below grade 1: Parking 104 parking spaces (312 total) 2: storage 3895 sq. Ft.

MARIPOSA AVENUE

section 12 Ft. above grade 1: ticket booth 2: giftshop 3: storage 4: giftshop 5: toilets library: 6: stacks A. audio-visual stacks 7: periodicals 8: classrooms 9: reading area 90 seats 10: reading rooms 11: AV viewing areas 12: AV listening areas 13: Xerox rooms 14: catalogs 15: children's library 16: Kimbank 17: staff work area 18: permanent collection galleries Prehistoric Korea ("antiquity") 19: permanent collection galleries Dynastic Korea ("Dynasty") 20: curator's suite 480 sq. Ft. 21: maintenance officers suite 480 sq. Ft. 22: security officers suite 480 sq. Ft. 23: storage 3895 sq. Ft.

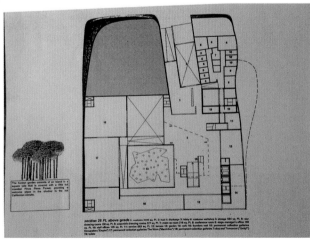

The Korean garden consists of an island in a square lake that is covered with a little but crooked Pinus Pinea Parasol, providing a welcome place in the shadow to the hot Californian climate.

section 20 Ft. above grade 1: costume 2400 sq. Ft. 2: bad 3: discharge 3: lobby 4: costume workshop & storage 504 sq. Ft. 5: star dressing rooms 120 sq. Ft. 6: ensemble dressing rooms 227 sq. Ft. 7: make-up room 216 sq. Ft. 8: conference room 9: stage manager's office 189 sq. Ft. 10: staff offices 126 sq. Ft. 11: service 503 sq. Ft. 12: terrace 13: garden 14: cafe 15: founders rest 16: permanent collection galleries Occupation ("Empire") 17: permanent collection galleries The Wars ("MacArthur") 18: permanent collection galleries Today and Tomorrow ("Unity") 19: toilets

234

section 38 Ft. above grade 1: temporary exhibition galleries 606 sq. Ft. 2: temporary exhibition galleries exhibition galleries 606 sq. Ft. 4: temporary exhibition galleries 606 sq. Ft. 5: foyer 541 sq.Ft. 6: foyer 2021 sq.Ft. 7: lobby

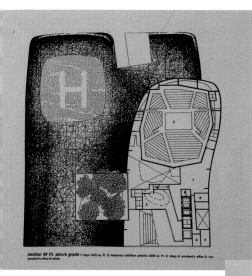

section 60 Ft. above grade 1: foyer 2435 sq. Ft. 2: temporary exhibition galleries 2596 sq. Ft. 3: stage 4: president's office 5: vice president's office 6: toilets

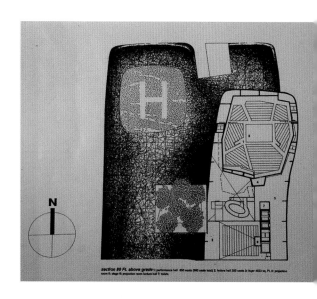

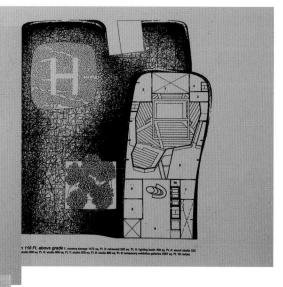

section 80 Ft. above grade 1: performance hall 650 seats (960 seats total) 2: lecture hall 200 seats 3: foyer 4823 sq. Ft. 4: projection room 5: stage 6: projection room lecture hall 7: toilets

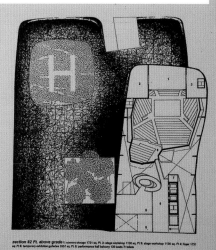

section 92 Ft. above grade 1: scenery storage 1731 sq. Ft. 2: stage workshop 1138 sq. Ft. 3: stage workshop 1138 sq. Ft. 4: foyer 1731 sq. Ft 5: temporary exhibition galleries 3887 sq. Ft. 6: performance hall balcony 130 seats 7: toilets

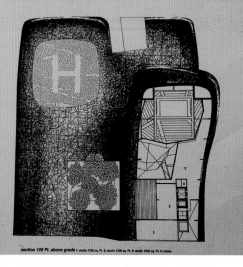

section 128 Ft. above grade 1: studio 1205 sq. Ft. 2: studio 1200 sq. Ft. 3: studio 3502 sq. Ft. 4: toilets

n 110 Ft. above grade 1: scenery storage 1472 sq. Ft. 2: rehearsal 800 sq. Ft. 3: lighting booth 498 sq. Ft. 4: sound studio 325 studio 600 sq. Ft. 6: studio 600 sq. Ft. 7: studio 520 sq. Ft. 8: studio 803 sq. Ft. 9: temporary exhibition galleries 2597 sq. Ft. 10: toilets

235

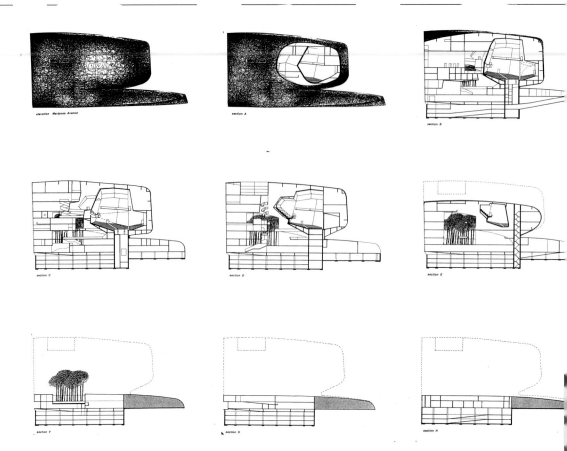

elevation Mariposa Avenue

section A

section B

section C

section D

section E

section F

section G

section H

When you are really serious in using a building to work on the public's image of a specific community, there is no getting round the icons of mass culture. After all, they define a great deal of the larger public's appreciation of facts and events. So the idea for our design for the Korean Museum of Modern Art and the route through it have both been derived from Disneyland Annaheim, the most popular amusement park in the region, more specifically from the roller coaster Space Mountain that had just been brought into use. The association with the microcosms of contradictions implied in the name 'Space Mountain' offered a splendid opportunity to explain the complexity and wealth of Korean culture to a broad and not always very educated public.

The exterior of our building is an icon, designed associatively. What one sees is a black granite sculpture, standing midway between a melted computer and a traditional granite Buddha. It is a closed object that at first sight confirms the prejudices playing a role in the racial rioting. But at the same time the building is like a sawn-through monolith, a rock in which geological layers and traces of life can be made out when sawn through and polished. A presse papier from souvenir shops. The interior explores various aspects of Korean culture. It is like an archaeological archive where different layers of history can be traced. Remains of various cultures from all the different eras of Korean history together form today's hybrid culture.

236

Firestation
Den Helder, 2006

239

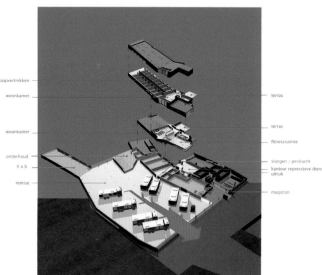

slaapvertrekken

woonkamer

woonkamer

onderhoud

h a b

remise

terras

terras

fitnessruimte

slangen / perslucht

kantoor repressieve dienst
uitruk

magazijn

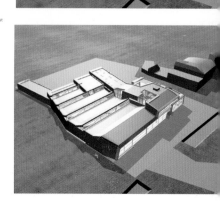

240

Fire station – the world of the fire brigade

The design for a fire station in a remote part of the Netherlands, is of a somewhat different order. In September 2001, when the attacks on the World Trade Center in New York took place, VenhoevenCS was commissioned to design a fire station for the Dutch town of Den Helder. Via the media, and particularly via television, it was clearly visible how heroic fire fighters approached near-certain death, driven by their rescue instincts. With the design for this station, we wished to offer insight into their world behind the scenes: the activities and everyday duties, the care for the equipment, and also how most fire fighters fulfil a boy's dream by almost blending with their machines and organization at certain moments.

241

Accordingly, the complex looks like a hangar that smells of oil and sweat. It is conspicuous and clearly recognizable from a distance. The building is modern, well prepared, and the smoothly running machine of the fire-fighting services nestles comfortably within the bodywork of the station. The entrance hall is separated from the fire engines by merely a glass partition, and is centrally situated in the building. On entering, visitors virtually find themselves right among the fire engines. This hall is a part of a larger space that extends up over several floors. Just as is the case with the heart of an organism, all the vital functions, such as the garage, warehouse, training areas, canteen, gym and lodgings, lie grouped around this hall.

242

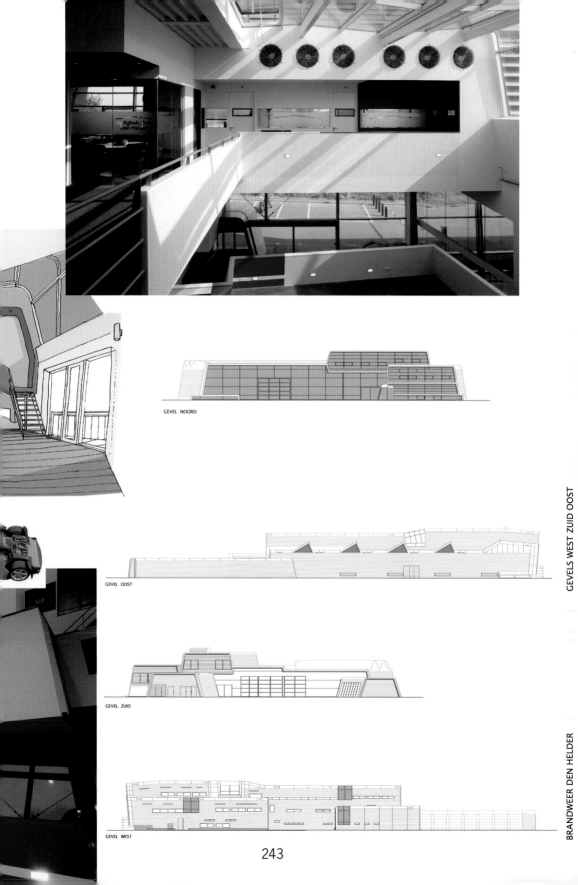

GEVEL NOORD

GEVEL OOST

GEVEL ZUID

GEVEL WEST

243

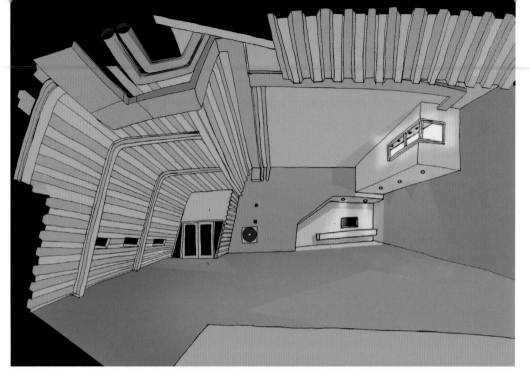

The interior cladding – the roof and the walls consist of profiled steel plating – has been left visible in the garage, the bedrooms and the working areas. Radiators, the steel construction, and also the pipes and ducts have been left visible, and various primary colours accentuate the machine-like character of the station. At the places where the fire-fighters cook, play cards, shower or sleep, the utilitarian interior has been equipped with a cladding of oak, synthetic material and stucco. This station is the skin of the fire-fighting services and a constituent of the equipment; the fire brigade is a heroic cyborg.

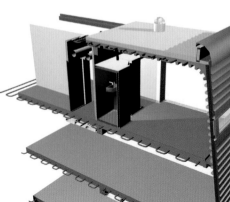

The Castle
Soest, 1992

248

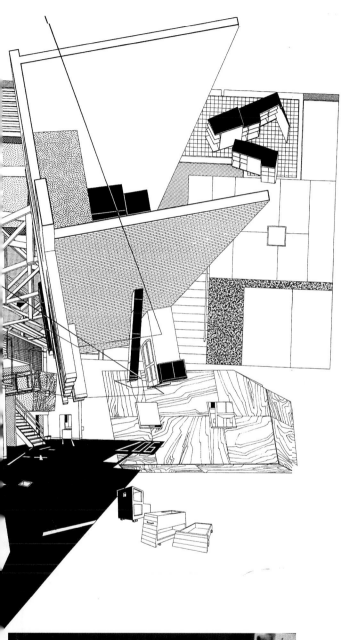

249

The Castle – the microcosm of a kindergarten

It was in the initial period of my firm when we were commissioned to design a day care and after-school child care centre to be built in a former domestic science school. That was a strange experience, for neither I myself nor the students partaking in the design had grown up in such a centre. Our references of places where you play and grow up went no further than: in the attic, under the table, in a farm barn and other informal places. Obviously there was a list of demands with the required number of square metres, but the very first thing we did was to supplement the list with the theoretical definition of a problem: suppose you place a 6 month-old child in a centre and it comes out again when twelve, has it developed independently to a sufficient degree in school and in the centre to function adequately in society? What must the design look like to achieve that result?

250

This led to an even more extreme question: suppose that the children never go outside – how to design an interior where they can flourish for twelve years? To get this done, we made frequent use of the combination of organization and disorientation. On one hand there are places for all sorts of regular activities with supervision, but there are also places where the children can experience the building as an endless accumulation of spaces. Here they can take risks, discover things and experience adventure. For very small children that possibility exists within the space of their own group, where the common space is surrounded by secret drawers, play corners and small flights of stairs. For the older children in the after-school child care centre, apart from their own living room, there is a complete labyrinth of high and low, long and bent spaces, different floor levels and stairs that they can use to their own liking. In addition they can play outside, of course.

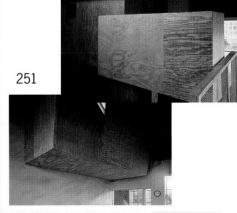

251

To make sure that children can discover new spaces and things in the same building for twelve years, we played with the relation between meaning and experience. What seems clear today may well play another role in a different context. And metamorphosis occurs everywhere: what starts as a wall, may turn into a box round the corner which one step further is transformed into a couch that eventually becomes a face. Objects and spaces appear, breathe and vanish. It is a folded space where stairs and bedrooms are intimately entwined – it is virtually impossible to see where one begins and the other stops. The interior appears fleshy and sculptural. Looking from one side, you think you see an object, whereas when looking from the other side it turns out not to exist. There is friction everywhere. As a child you are often left empty-handed. You have to find your own way. You cannot reduce forms to a notion without finding that the next day they will challenge you to put a different name to them. This project cannot possibly be photographed.'[56]

(56)
THE CASTLE
'Then we set to work, worked on the result and worked on it again, until the ideas were grown together with new ones like rhizomes. Eventually we found ourselves back in a world of danger, comfort, risk, excitement and homeliness. Sometimes it looks as if the building is infinitely complex, sometimes it appears open and impertinent. It can grow in the child's head, for twelve years. There are spaces of one metre, ten centimetres and ten metres high. There are dirty rooms, soft walls, clean, funny or incomprehensible things.' Ton Venhoeven

252

Community school Forum 't Zand
Utrecht, 2005

Forum 't Zand – village in a spaceship

The idea of the community school came from Sweden, There, it is a place children go to and where they receive lessons, alternated with play. The day is not divided according to the traditional schedule. Some of the pupils get classes in the mornings, while other children are playing and vice versa. The result is a kind of village in which teaching and play are divided over the day as in normal life. Apart from being a school, the village is a playground and a community centre as well.

In the Netherlands, community schools are often used to bring children from diverse cultural backgrounds together. More and more parents have children when they are getting older and regard them as little princes or princesses, with all its consequences. Rather than being part of large families as in the past, children are more often than not at home alone or with one other sibling, living in their own cultural capsules. The community school is a means of ensuring that such children meet 'other' children, that is, children whose positions in life are different. They may also be regarded as special spaces, in which all children and parents may jointly be seen as forming an experimental garden for society at large, their interiors are a kind of pressure cookers. Relationships that occur less and less frequently in society are cultivated in the microcosms of their interiors.

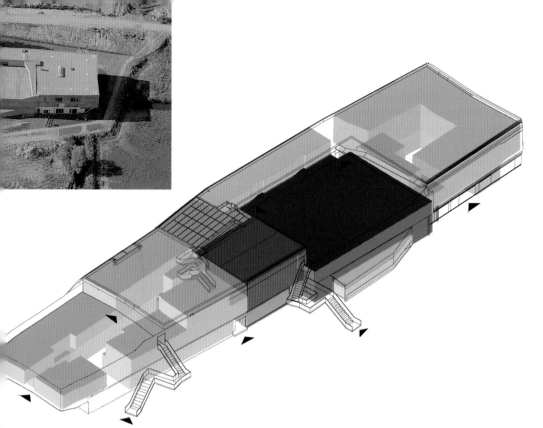

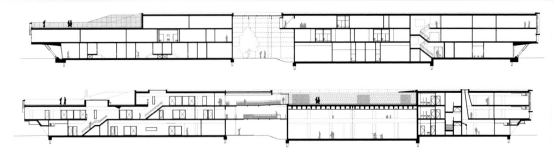

The original programme of requirements was a combination of entities, comprising a traditional and a Montessori-based primary school, a day nursery, a playgroup, a community centre with social amenities, a sports centre and a youth welfare centre. One of the challenges we faced was to find out whether the inter-space could be used by creating clever dual functions. One cluster of functions found its place around the entrance, comprising a bar, a meeting room, a winter garden, a gymnasium and an extracurricular centre, all in one place. We tried to find ways of saving place by having different users occupy the same spaces at different times. By dividing the building up as effectively as possible we even had spare space for a winter garden with plants and trees.

Initially, we looked for a campus-type model, with separate pavilions. However, that proved infeasible. There were insufficient funds for all the additional facades, stairwells and cloakrooms that would be required. We therefore opted for the opposite approach: as wide a building as possible, with a minimum of facade, stairwells and cloakrooms. Less facade is not only advantageous in terms of building costs, but also in terms of energy management. A number of playgrounds were situated on the roof, providing a saving in land costs and, in addition, obviating the need for fencing. As a result the school grounds became the extension of an adjacent park.

A community school should not look like a large school. Children spend twelve years of their lives at school and there is more to those lives than education alone. In this light, the idea of a spaceship was developed. Spaceships play a prominent part in children's visual imagination. In this case the spaceship would play the part of a galactic Noah's Ark, accommodating an entire children's village, with all its different spaces. The spaceship would be bound on a voyage lasting many years and the children would have to survive for generations, breeding animals and growing plants. This idea remained our source of inspiration.

262

The spaceship itself appeals to the world of games, films and exciting stories. It is more fun to enter a rocket than to go to school. This is certainly the case if the rocket has made an emergency landing in your neighbourhood and its lowered flight stairs are reminiscent of the headlong evacuation of aliens. Judging by its exterior, the rocket has been through many adventures. Maybe it will suddenly take off tomorrow, just like that.

Designing is partly a matter of staging. A decor of daily life is constructed but need not always be constructed in material form. Staging allows one to intervene in the virtual space of the image culture. Designs are not only about how space works in terms of volume, but also about how it works on the surface and what impressions are created. The present building is not marked by just a single characteristic. On the contrary, it is capable of assuming many different characters. It is interactive and based on traditional features, involving spaces, relieved surfaces, light, patterns and colours.

The interior of the building contains as many differently shaped spaces as possible. The children's places are on different scales, sometimes intimate and safe, at other times large and adventurous, just as in the 'real' world. Differently coloured planes are applied in the rooms, allowing the occupants to make up stories on the basis of the patterns. In fact, colours and patterns are not used to explain the building but to allow for new interpretations.

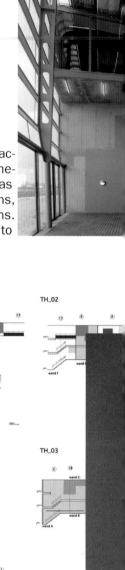

264

265

zuidgevel

noordgevel

ventilatieopening achter gevel (moet
achter plaat met 1/& perforatie vallen)
+ clustering buitenverlichting in aluminium
cassette (88 stuks)

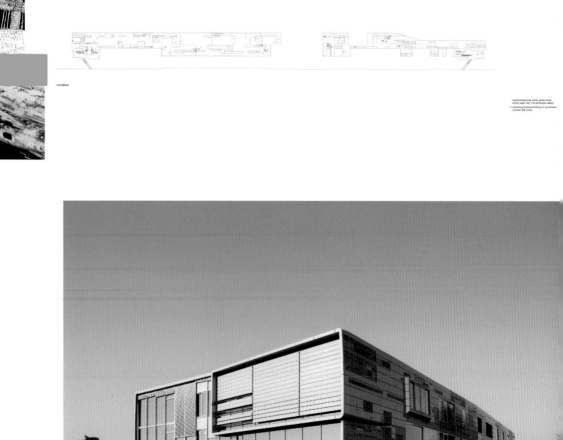

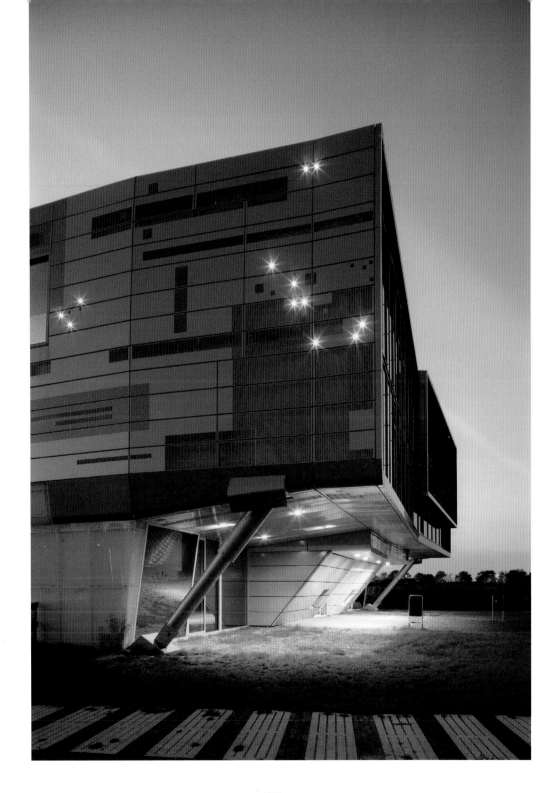

271

European Patent Office – an autarkic subject

The future will bring us fully autarkic, even energy and food producing buildings and cities. No more fossil fuels are needed, buildings and cities produce enough energy, even to drive cars and fly aeroplanes. They produce their own food and recycle enough materials to renew buildings when needed. The ecological footprint of such cities is equal to their own surface.

272   Since the European Patent Office is specialized in registering the most advanced inventions, the competition for a new building for this organization offered a good opportunity to stimulate the development of such buildings and cities.

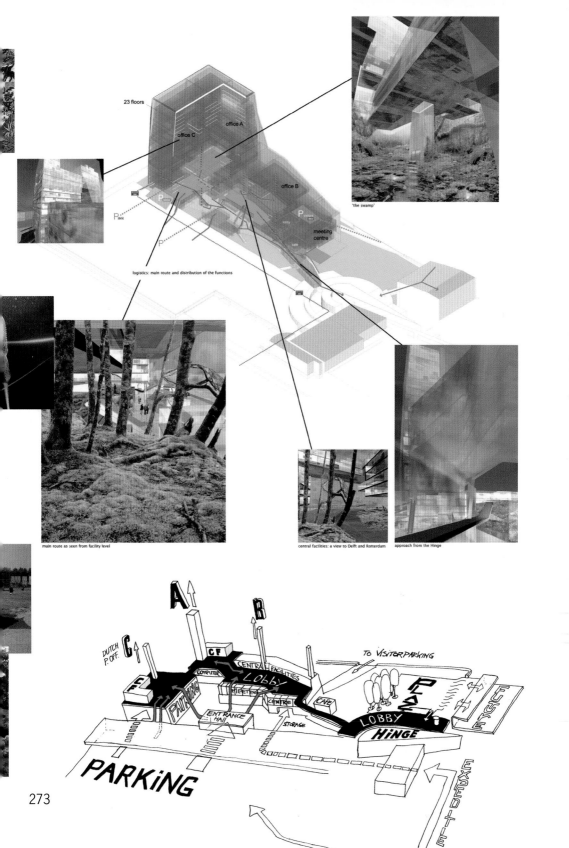

23 floors

office A

office C

office B

'the swamp'

logistics: main route and distribution of the functions

meeting centre

main route as seen from facility level

central facilities: a view to Delft and Rotterdam

approach from the Hinge

DUTCH P. OFF. C

A

B

TO VISITOR PARKING

CF

CENTRAL FACILITIES

COMPUTER

LOBBY

PARKING

MEETING

CENTRE

CAFE

LOBBY

HINGE

ENTRANCE HALL

STORAGE

PARKING

EXPEDITIE

EMPLOYEES TO PARKING

273

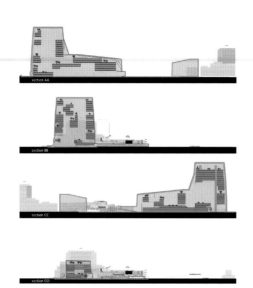

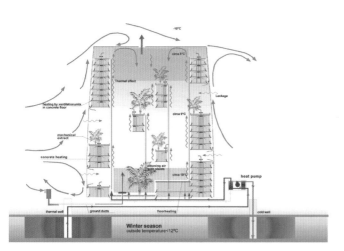

Winter season
outside temperature<12°C

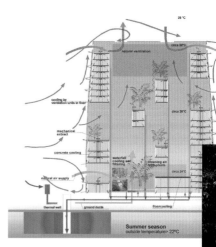

Summer season
outside temperature> 22°C

Our proposal is an invention or prototype, rather than just a design for another building. The basic idea has drawn its inspiration from the hanging gardens of Babylon and from the experiments with biospheres of the seventies and eighties of the last century.[57,58] It is a kind of glasshouse, a glass body in which offices, gardens, sports facilities, restaurants, a desert bar and a river are combined. Depending on the climate of the specific place in the building, there are tropical, subtropical or desert gardens. These provide a combination of biotopes in the building. Depending on the weather conditions one can work or have meetings in the gardens.[59]

(57)
DEVONIAN GARDENS
A contemporary example of indoor hanging gardens can be visited in Canada, where a 2.5 acre climate controlled garden can be found on the 4th floor of an office building and shopping centre in downtown Calgary, Alberta. The gardens feature more than 138 varieties of plants. The design includes an entrance gate, a Quiet Garden, a woodland setting, waterfalls, fountains, koi and turtle pools and a Sun Garden.

(58)
BIOSPHERE
Biosphere 2, was built in Oracle Arizona (USA) between 1987 and 1991 as an artificial, closed ecological system. With its size of 3.14 acre, it contained a miniature rainforest, an ocean with coral reef of 850 m², mangrove wetlands, 1,900 m²'s of savannah grassland, a fog desert and an agricultural system. It was used to study and understand the complex web of interactions between different life systems in earth's real biosphere (biosphere 1) for ecological purposes, but also to be able to colonize space in the future. Check the Internet!

(59)
BIOTOPE
A biotope is an area of, depending on scale, more or less uniform environmental conditions that provide a li[...] place for a specific combinatio[...] of plants and animals. The word 'b[...]otope' is strongly related to the ter[...] 'ecosystem', which is generally used [...] reflect on a larger scale.

274

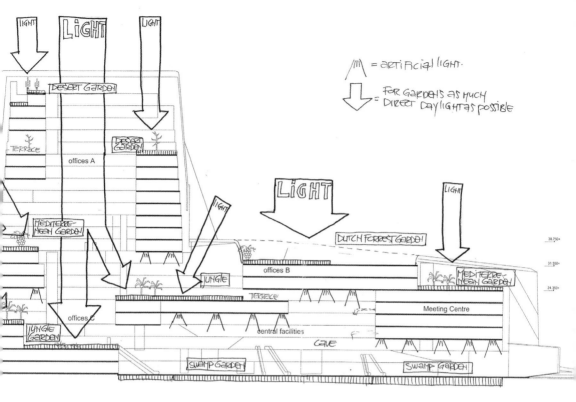

LighT

LighT

LighT

/||| = artificial light.

⬇ = For gardens as much Direct daylight as possible

DESERT GARDEN

TERRACE

offices A

DESERT GARDEN

MEDITERRE-NEAN GARDEN

LighT

LighT

DUTCH FORREST GARDEN

offices B

JUNGLE

MEDITERRE-NEAN GARDEN

38.750+

31.550+

24.350+

TERRACE

Meeting Centre

offices C

JUNGLE GARDEN

central facilities

CAVE

SWAMP GARDEN

SWAMP GARDEN

-A   Section A-A   Coupe A-A

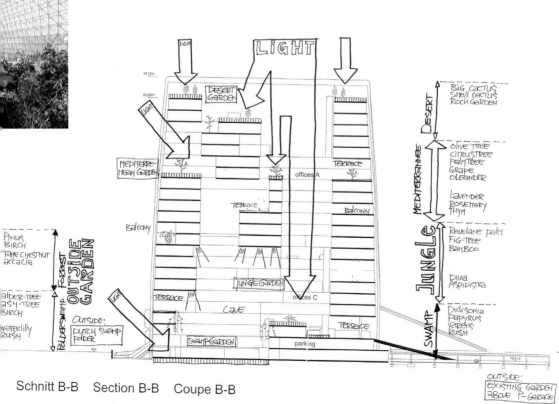

lighT

LighT

68.755+

62.000+

DESERT GARDEN

LighT

MEDITERRE-NEAN GARDEN

TERRACE

offices A

DESERT

Big CACTUS
small CACTUS
Rock GARDEN

OUVE TREE
CITRUS TREE
PALM TREE
GRAPE
OLEANDER

lavender
ROSEMARY
THYM

MEDITERRANEAN

Balcony

TERRACE

Balcony

PINUS
BIRCH
TRUE CHESTNUT
accacia

Balcony

RAVENANE PALM
FIG-TREE
BAMBOO

JUNGLE

ALDER-TREE
ASH-TREE
BIRCH

OUTSIDE GARDEN

ALDER SWAMP FOREST

JUNGLE GARDEN

offices C

DIVIA
ASPIDISTRA

WATERLILLY
RUSH

OUTSIDE:
DUTCH SWAMP Folder

TERRACE

CAVE

TERRACE

DICKSONIA
PAPYRUS
VARENS
RUSH

SWAMP

SWAMP GARDEN

parking

45°

REF:0

OUTSIDE:
EXISTING GARDEN
ABOVE P-GARAGE

Schnitt B-B   Section B-B   Coupe B-B

According to independent cost calculations, a futuristic design like this is feasible because it works as an autarkic system; the building can function without the supply of food and external energy, which saves a lot of money over the years. We only applied available technical possibilities in the design. A climate skin with integrated solar energy collectors provides a pleasant climate while retaining the physical experience of the changing seasons. Every space is ventilated in a natural way and many are in direct contact with a garden. Even on the twentieth floor the sliding door of an office can be opened to enjoy a subtropical garden.

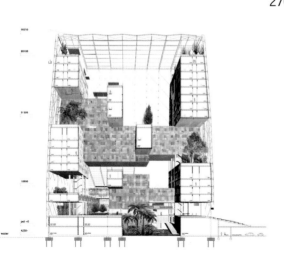

We aimed to design a truly futuristic building: not by playing into the utopian or distopian views of the future of our culture as is common in B-films and games, but with a vision of the future in which the building would be a popular place to be by combining the functions of everyday life with leisure, excitement and a certain amount of discomfort and adventure. In theory such an approach, where different things happen in each other's vicinity, also saves time, mobility and energy. To get in the right mood, we watched science fiction films such as <u>M e t r o p o l i s</u> and <u>S t a r   W a r s</u> to draw inspiration from.

When one enters the building on the ground floor, no offices are visible. The complex might as well be a deserted, extraterrestrial construction. To achieve this effect, we came up with a specific detailing of windows, elevations and ceilings. Due to a <u>p a t c h w o r k</u> of perforations in plates and by printing patterns on windows, the building loses its scale. It could be a kilometre high. There are windows that do not want to be windows, elevations that refuse to be elevations. Every distinction between window, floor and elevation, and every sense of scale to hold on, has gone.

City of cities
Chungcheongnam, 2005

280

Environmental issues become ever more pressing, also in city design. After all, when you include the traffic that city planning creates, current cities consume some seventy or eighty percent of total energy production worldwide. A contemporary design for a city should therefore aim at nothing less than total autarky when it comes to energy and food production. The only way to develop a sustainable culture with a growing world populations eager to adapt to a cosmopolitan lifestyle, is to make the footprint of each city equal to its own ecological footprint.[60] Sufficient energy production can be reached by making energy efficient cities and buildings and covering facades with printed solar cells, turning every single building into a power plant. Food can be produced on allotments, roofs and in buildings, by means of urban agriculture. Sufficient production can take place within the city limits.

7.15 am   7.30 am   8.00 am   8.45 am   6.00 pm   7.30 pm   8.45 pm

We took this basic idea as a starting point for the design of the new South Korean city of Chungcheongnam. Apart from being a solution to local requirements, our design is also a prototype that should be developed further, its principle can be adapted everywhere. There is no dominant identity or atmosphere in this city nor does it need a specific political organization. Therefore it suits every political system.

(60)
ECOLOGICAL FOOTPRINT
The ecological footprint compares human demand of resources with planet Earth's ecological capacity to regenerate the resources and deal with the waste, given prevailing technology and resource management practice.
Wackernagel and Rees, Our Ecological Footprint: Reducing Human Impact on the Earth'(Gabriola Island, BC: New Society Publishers, 1996)
Check the Internet for calculating your own footprint!

We took the best possible combination of two different traditions of city development. The self-organizing city and the centrally planned city. A self-organizing city grows spontaneously from the moment people start building huts and shantytowns and can develop into a full grown mega-polis. In the process such a city develops millions of micro networks that use and reuse all opportunities that the flowering city tissue offers. This type of city is surprisingly sustainable, as if it is a self-sufficient biotope.

The centrally planned city on the other hand may offer a better quality of life, but it often uses an incredible amount of energy. This is due to the zoning laws that prohibit different activities to mix. You have to use your car to go from your work to your house, to pick up your kids, to go to your fitness centre, to a restaurant, or to go shopping. This is all not very convenient or sustainable and it requires a lot of natural resources.

Our city design or prototype is neither strictly planned in its building volumes, nor do we propose a spontaneous development over time. It will develop parts that resemble the most populated areas of Hong Kong and parts that make one think of suburban areas of Australia and everything in between. Within the restrictions of its strictly defined outer borders and inner infrastructure, buildings and neighbourhoods grow where the circumstances of location and infrastructure are favourable. People, buildings and neighbourhoods live of each other. Other than maximum heights to guarantee different types of light penetration in different areas, no zoning law is required. Spaces that must remain open for sports and leisure, simply have a maximum height of zero.

Variation in the city islands is created by an irregular grid of main roads and side-roads. There are extra large and large, but also medium sized and small low-traffic islands in this urban archipelago. This way, everybody can find a location to their taste. The new version of the city block is not a mono functional island, but a micro city, village or metropolis. It is possible for each island to have a varying programme and a different development density. There can be schools, offices, houses, businesses and shops side by side with special public spaces, casual interspaces, squares, parks, streets, alleys and playgrounds.

283

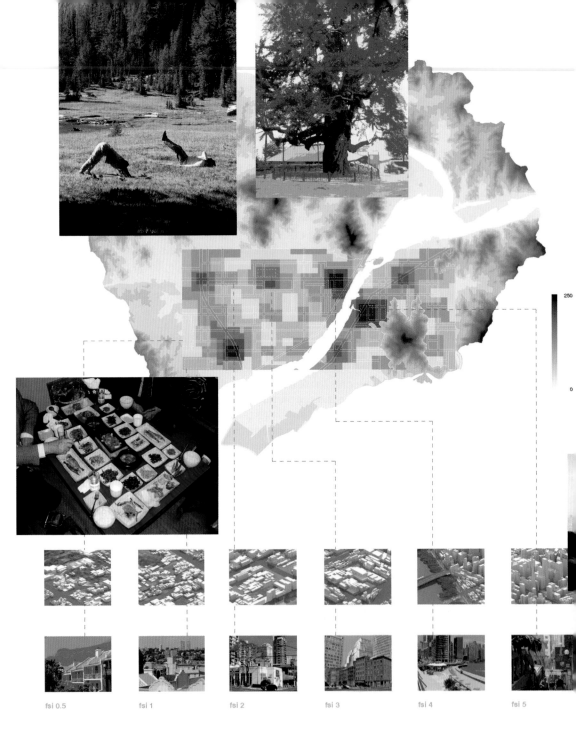

fsi 0.5   fsi 1   fsi 2   fsi 3   fsi 4   fsi 5

Together the islands form configurations of micro networks connecting different districts. Some activities occur in each block and some in a few; others only once in the entire city. The islands and micronetworks are interconnected by pedestrian routes traversing the whole city. By way of these routes, all parks and other areas of natural beauty are also within reach, like the ones situated by the river, on the hills and outside the city.

dential area
ro stop
c complex
lth care
lic services
gion
ure
ure
rts facilities
k / agriculture
isteries
ces
nesses
nairy school
ondary school
ege / university
pping neighbourhood level
pping city level
a (78 km2)

285

In the urban fabric side-streets, main roads and urban motorways are woven into the city's tissue. The smaller ones of these streets define the outlines of the islands, big ones occasionally dive under or fly over the city tissue to prevent disconnecting the micro networks that feed the city. Our Chungcheongnam possesses a public transport system with an underground and a suspended railway, regional railway connections and a junction with the high-speed train. Where various traffic systems converge, metropolitan junctions are created. Everything is so close together that one can practically do without the car. Most village, urban and metropolitan areas are at walking distance from each other.

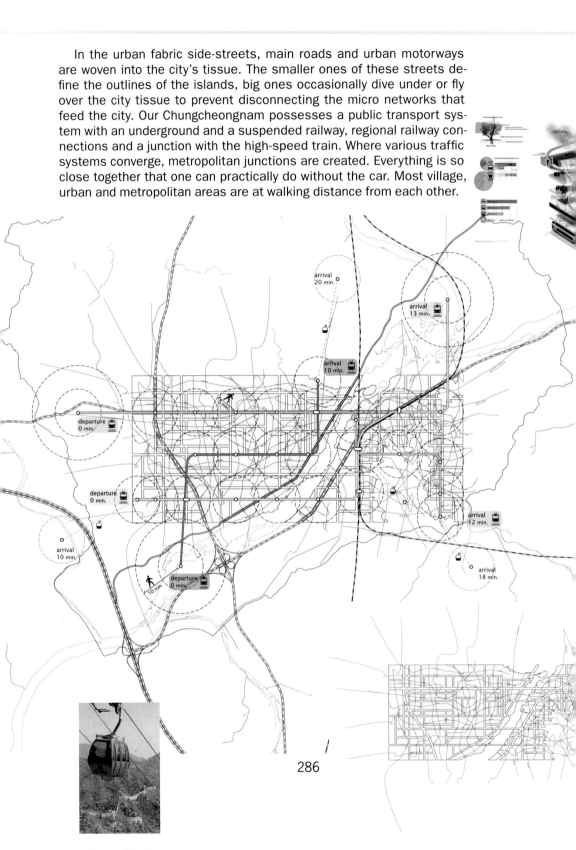

286

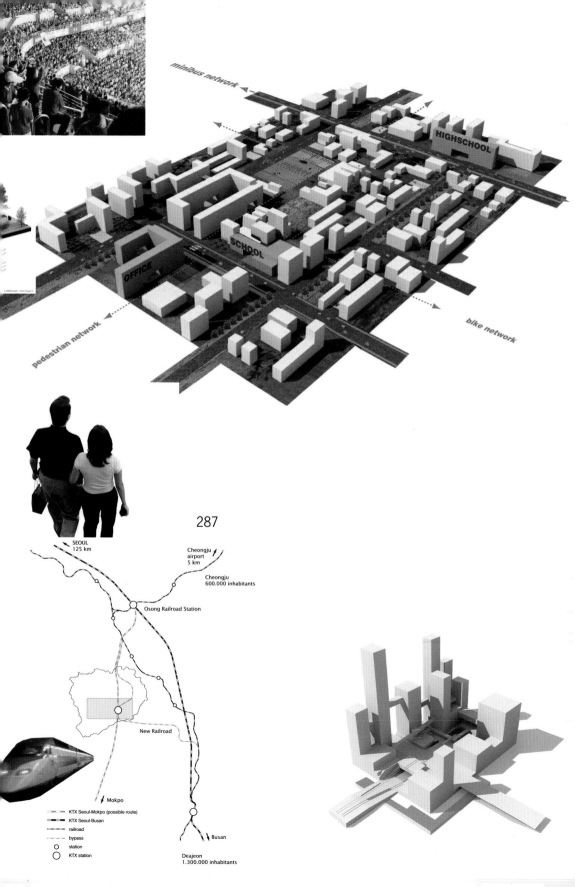

minibus network

HIGHSCHOOL

SCHOOL

OFFICE

pedestrian network

bike network

287

SEOUL
125 km

Cheongju
airport
5 km

Cheongju
600.000 inhabitants

Osong Railroad Station

New Railroad

Mokpo

━━━ KTX Seoul-Mokpo (possible route)
━━━ KTX Seoul-Busan
━━━ railroad
━━━ bypass
○ station
◯ KTX station

Busan

Deajeon
1.300.000 inhabitants

In this design 18 out of the 73 available square kilometres are used for 500,000 inhabitants and 200,000 work places. Including the other functions, this comes down to an average density comparable with that of Paris within the Boulevard Périphérique.

We do not need the remaining fifty-five square kilometres, so they are returned to nature, which is never farther away than one and a half kilometres, about a quarter of an hour's walk or a few minutes by underground or aerial railway. This new area of natural beauty outside the city will be arranged in such a way that nature is able to regain it as a biotope for wildlife.

List of works

oating Skyscraper
ngapore (SG)

G Area
nsterdam (NL)

O 9. Zeeburg
nsterdam (NL)

udio
ageningen (NL)

rt Asperen
peren (NL)

FONS WELTERS
AMSTERDAM (NL)
1988 (proposal)
Art Gallery
200 m²
Ton Venhoeven

VENDEXDRIEHOEK
AMSTERDAM (NL)
1989 (study)
Shopping mall; supermarket, shops,
apartments, bars, restaurants, roof
garden, parking garage
25,000 m²
Ton Venhoeven, Arend Rutgers, Joost
van Veen, Dorothee Stürmer

FLOATING SKYSCRAPER
SINGAPORE (SG)
1989 (study)
Geostationary skyscraper
71,572 kilometres high
Ton Venhoeven

WG AREA
AMSTERDAM (NL)
1990 – 1993 (realized)
45 apartments for elderly people and
police station
5,400 m²
Ton Venhoeven, Cas Bollen, Arend
Rutgers, Joost van Veen, Vania from
Brasil, in collaboration with artist
Aernout Mik

MELKWEG
AMSTERDAM (NL)
1990 (proposal)
Art installation in music centre
100 m²
Ton Venhoeven

FAMILY DE KROON
LEIDSCHENDAM (NL)
1990 (realized)
Home refurbishment
100 m²
Ton Venhoeven

HET KASTEEL
SOEST (NL)
1991 – 1992 (realized)
Conversion of domestic science
school; day care centre,
extracurricular child nursery
2,000 m²
Ton Venhoeven, Daan Bakker, Kirsten
van den Berg, Matthijs Bouw, Mirjam
Galjé

CHRISTIES
AMSTERDAM (NL)
1991 (realized)
Café interior
300 m²
Ton Venhoeven, Arend Rutgers

BIJLMER TUNNEL
AMSTERDAM (NL)
1992 (study)
Tunnel renovation and public space
5,100 m²
Ton Venhoeven

HEIJPLAAT
ROTTERDAM (NL)
1993 – 1994 (realized in a one day
event)
Playground for children from 0-18
years old; playing objects, special
features, landscape design
10,000 m²
Ton Venhoeven, Marco Vermeulen,
Ronald Wall, and international
students of Workship Holland, Nancy
Kruytzer, Menno van der Woude, in
collaboration with artist Aernout Mik

RONALD MCDONALD HOUSE
UTRECHT (NL)
1993 (proposal)
Hotel and care centre
2,500 m²
Ton Venhoeven, Joost Ector

PLETTENBURG DE WIERS
NIEUWEGEIN (NL)
1993 (proposal)
Art installation
2 m²
Ton Venhoeven, in collaboration with
artist Aernout Mik

NO 9. ZEEBURG
AMSTERDAM (NL)
1994 (study)
Housing block; apartments for elderly
people
3,124 m²
Ton Venhoeven, Kirsten van den Berg

STUDIO
WAGENINGEN (NL)
1994 (proposal)
Studio for graphic designer
60 m²
Ton Venhoeven, Nancy Kruytzer

GEINWIJK
AMSTERDAM (NL)
1995 – 1998 (realized)
Housing project; 101 houses, 23
apartments
11,160 m²
Ton Venhoeven, Mirjam Galjé, Cas
Bollen, in collaboration with artist
Marc Ruygrok

KOMA
LOS ANGELES (USA)
1995 (study)
Korean museum and cultural centre;
exhibition spaces, entrance hall,
foyer, auditorium, storage spaces,
workshops, studios for artists in
residence, bar, restaurant, offices,
loading dock
25,034 m²
Ton Venhoeven, Tom Frantzen, Mirjam
Galjé, Jules van Vark

OOSTELIJKE HANDELSKADE
AMSTERDAM (NL)
1995 (study)
Urban planning; apartments, studios,
offices, workshops, parking, public
spaces
500,000 m²
Ton Venhoeven, Miranda Nieboer,
Gerard van Heel

RIETLANDEN
AMSTERDAM (NL)
1995 – 2001 (realized)
Housing project; 156 apartments,
studios, parking garages, medical
practice, public space
28,523 m²
Ton Venhoeven, Peter Heideman,
Arjen Zaal, Cas Bollen, Mirjam Galjé,
André de Ruiter, Jules van Vark, Jen
Alkema, Miranda Nieboer, Bart van
den Berg, Peter Baas, Chantal van
Dillen, John Daas, Jeroen Tacx, Henk
van der Woude, Gjermund Kiserud

DE GRAAF HOUSE
TERSCHELLING (NL)
1995 (study)
Holiday home; extension
24 m²
Ton Venhoeven

DE VLEESHAL
MIDDELBURG (NL)
1996 (realized)
Art installation; slideshow and
publication
Ton Venhoeven, in collaboration with
artist Ronald van Tienhoven

FORT ASPEREN
ASPEREN (NL)
1997 (realized at International Art
Exhibition)
Temporary art installation
100 m²
Ton Venhoeven, Arjen Zaal, in
collaboration with artist Aernout Mik

U2 GEUZENVELD
AMSTERDAM (NL)
1997 – 2001 (realized)
50 units for elderly psychiatric
patients, 39 apartments for elderly
people, 4 apartments for
handicapped people, 4 houses, 2
shops and supermarket
9,000 m²
Ton Venhoeven, Pascal Bemelmans,
Mirjam Galjé, Vincent de Graaf,
Gerald Lindner, Arjen Zaal, Erik de
Vries, Peterine Arts, Mike Korth, Bas
Römgens

JAN SCHAEFER BRIDGE
AMSTERDAM (NL)
1997 – 2001 (realized)
Bridge for cars, bicycles, pedestrians,
285 m.
Ton Venhoeven, Bart Aptroot, Mirjam
Galjé, Cas Bollen, Mark Linneman,
Beat Ferrario, Paul Landman, Knut
Kruse, Arjen Zaal, Matthijs Klooster,
Chantal van Dillen, in collaboration
with artists Marc Ruygrok and Aernout
Mik

DE ZWIJGER
AMSTERDAM (NL)
1997 – 2000 (proposal)
Cultural centre, conversion of
warehouse; foyer, theatres,
workspaces, shops, bars
6,000 m²
Ton Venhoeven, Mike Korth, Jeroen
Tacx, Jos-Willem van Oorschot

HOUSING
WAGENINGEN (NL)
1997 (proposal)
Urban plan; houses, apartments
and shops
8,000 m²
Ton Venhoeven, Arjen Zaal

LABORATORY, FOOD AND
PRODUCT SAFETY AUTHORITY
ZWIJNDRECHT (NL)
1998 – 2003 (realized)
Laboratory building; offices,
laboratories, research halls, parking
garage
6,400 m²
Ton Venhoeven, Kees Plomp, Beate
Lendt, Chantal van Dillen, Jos-Willem
van Oorschot, Björn Utpott, Peter
Heideman, Jeroen Tacx, Katie
Cassidy, Erwin Hilbrands

BLASIO
ROTTERDAM (NL)
1998 (realized)
Jumping cushion to celebrate the
tenth anniversary of the Netherlands
Architecture Institute (NAi)
36 m² x 3 metres
Ton Venhoeven, Bart Aptroot, Chantal
van Dillen

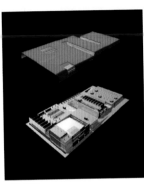

Mega 2
Rome (I)

Car mall
Zwijndrecht (NL)

Music Centre Enschede
Enschede (NL)

EVE
NEW YORK (USA)
1998 (study)
Park and sports centre; public park,
sports facilities, parking garage,
supermarket, health centre, spa, day
care centre, nightclub, shops, bars
100,000 m²
Ton Venhoeven, Chantal van Dillen,
Jos-Willem van Oorschot, Silvia Forlati

MEGA 2
ROME (I)
October 1998 (study)
Conference, trade and exhibition
centre; auditoriums, exhibition
spaces, offices, bars, restaurants,
shops and parking garage
150,000 m²
Ton Venhoeven, Chantal van Dillen,
Jos-Willem van Oorschot, Silvia Forlati

U3, DE DRIE BOUWMEESTERS
AMSTERDAM (NL)
1998 – 2006 (realized)
Housing project and urban planning;
44 houses, 39 apartments, car park,
landscape design
15,727 m²
Ton Venhoeven, Arjen Zaal, Chantal
van Dillen, Erik de Vries, Pascal
Bemelmans, Bas Römgens, Pieter
Lievense, in collaboration with artist
Arno van der Mark

DONGEZONE
TILBURG (NL)
1999 – 2001 (proposal)
Urban planning and housing project;
99 houses, 44 apartments, parking
garage, underground street,
landscape design
4.1 hectare, 38,700 m²
Ton Venhoeven, Bart Aptroot, Danny
Esselman, Peterine Arts, Jos- Willem
van Oorschot, Ton Span, Anna
Lacerda, Catarina Crespo, in
collaboration with artist Arno van der
Mark

TUNNEL BOULEVARD HOUTHAVENS
AMSTERDAM (NL)
1999 – 2003 (proposal)
Tunnel with boulevard and bridges
Overall length 550 metres
Ton Venhoeven, Jos-Willem van
Oorschot, Mike Korth, Peterine Arts,
Chantal van Dillen

CRUQUIUSWEG I
AMSTERDAM (NL)
1999 – 2000 (study)
Industry and living; apartments, office
spaces, supermarket, collective park,
indoor harbour, facilities, parking
garage
166,000 m²
Ton Venhoeven, Jos-Willem van
Oorschot, Bas Römgens, Arjen Zaal

VAN DIEMENSTRAAT
AMSTERDAM (NL)
1999 – 2000 (study)
Tunnel with multipurpose building;
tunnel, apartments, shops, office
space, facilities and parking garage
39,000 m² + tunnel
Ton Venhoeven, Jos-Willem van
Oorschot, Chantal van Dillen, Bas
Römgens

VENHOEVENCS
AMSTERDAM (NL)
1999 (realized)
Architectural office and workshop
interior
560 m²
Ton Venhoeven, Peterine Arts

TERWIJDE
UTRECHT (NL)
2000 (proposal)
Urban plan and housing project;
apartments, villa's, facilities, parking
garage, garden
14,850 m²
Ton Venhoeven, Peterine Arts, Arjen
Zaal

CAR MALL
ZWIJNDRECHT (NL)
2000 (study)
Urban planning of business centre for
car dealers; showrooms, repair
workshops, supply rooms, storage
space, offices, car park
79,500 m²
Ton Venhoeven, Kees Plomp, Peterine
Arts, Jos-Willem van Oorschot, Pieter
Lievense

CRUQUIUS II
AMSTERDAM (NL)
2001 – 2002 (study)
Multipurpose building; business
accommodation, office spaces,
business apartments, shops, bars,
restaurants, studios, parking garage
17,386 m²
Ton Venhoeven, Jos-Willem van
Oorschot, Peterine Arts, Arjen Zaal

MUSIC CENTRE ENSCHEDE
ENSCHEDE (NL)
2001 (study)
Music centre; auditoriums, foyers,
rehearsal rooms, workshops, offices,
loading dock
18,000 m²
Ton Venhoeven, Jos-Willem van
Oorschot

FORUM 'T ZAND
UTRECHT (NL)
2001 – 2005 (realized)
Community school; public elementary
school, Montessori elementary
school, day care centres,
extracurricular spaces, leisure centre,
sports centre, foyer, bar, winter
garden
7,100 m²
Ton Venhoeven, Erwin Hilbrands,
Peterine Arts, Erik de Vries, Cécilia
Gross, Kees Plomp, Jos-Willem van
Oorschot, Xander Bernaards

SPORTPLAZA MERCATOR
AMSTERDAM (NL)
2001 – 2006 (realized)
Multipurpose sports and cultural
community centre; 25 metres
competition pool, therapy pool,
multipurpose pool, outdoor pool,
recreation pools, fitness rooms, spa,
bar, restaurant, multipurpose party
halls, kindergarten, fast-food
restaurant, sun terrace and park
7,100 m²
Ton Venhoeven, Richèl Lubbers,
Danny Esselman, Jos-Willem van
Oorschot, Erik de Vries, Thomas
Flotmann, Michael Schwaiger,
Manfred Wansink, Kerstin Nigsch,
Unai Fdz.de Betoño, Andrea Alvarez,
Mustafa Karagoz, Peterine Arts, in
collaboration with artist Giny Vos

ARCAM
AMSTERDAM (NL)
2001 (realized)
Exhibition
100 m²
Ton Venhoeven, Aukje van Bezeij, in
collaboration with photographer
Marjoleine Boonstra

SUBWAY
BUILDING LEEUWARDERWEG
AMSTERDAM (NL)
2001 (study)
Urban plan for the development of a
subway station; station, offices,
shops, apartments, leisure facilities
35,000 m²
Ton Venhoeven

HOUSING
HEERHUGOWAARD (NL)
2002 (study)
Urban plan and landscape design;
houses, apartments, mobile homes,
sports centre, facilities, park, forest
29 hectare
Ton Venhoeven, Peterine Arts, in
collaboration with Alle Hosper, office
for landscape design

LYCEUM
HAARLEM (NL)
2002 (study)
School for lower secondary
professional education; school,
parking garage
12,000 m²
Ton Venhoeven, Jos-Willem van
Oorschot

FIRE STATION
DEN HELDER (NL)
2002 – 2007 (realized)
Fire station; garage, repair
workshops, supply rooms, offices,
classrooms, canteen, fitness room,
living rooms, bedrooms, bar, practice
room, car park, exercise area
5,100 m²
Ton Venhoeven, Peter Heideman,
Kees Plomp, Erik de Vries, Danny
Esselman, Ton Span, Mendel
Robbers, Bas Römgens, Jos-Willem
van Oorschot, Sebastian Kutschki

KOOIPLEIN
LEIDEN (NL)
2002 – 2006 (proposal)
Urban plan and tunnel; tunnel,
houses, apartments, supermarket,
shops, studios, office spaces, care
centre, police station, community
centre, community school, theatre,
mosque, housing for elderly people,
parking garage, park
110,000 m², 16 hectare
Ton Venhoeven, Arjen Zaal, Danny
Esselman, Michael Schwaiger, Bas
Römgens, Jos-Willem van Oorschot,
in collaboration with urban planner
Rients Dijkstra and Maxwan

FIRE STATION LEIDSCHE RIJN
UTRECHT (NL)
2002 (study)
Fire station; garage, workshops,
storage rooms, fitness room, offices,
living room, bedrooms, exercise
rooms, canteen
5,000 m²
Ton Venhoeven, Arjen Zaal, Jos-
Willem van Oorschot in collaboration
with artist Marten Winters

iversity of Groningen (RUG)
oningen (NL)

n Hasseltkanaal
nsterdam (NL)

uwersoog
e Marne (NL)

...crystals. Spatially mapping the...
pseudomolecular and fragmentions of the...

M AMOLF
nsterdam (NL)

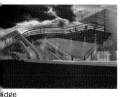

dge
orn (NL)

PIG HOUSE
TILBURG (NL)
2002 (study)
High-tech, sustainable pig house
Various sizes
Ton Venhoeven

COMMUNITY CENTRE
NIJMEGEN (NL)
2002 (study)
Arts and community centre and
school; elementary schools, arts
centre, auditorium, apartments,
houses
24,000 m²
Ton Venhoeven, Arjen Zaal, Jos-
Willem van Oorschot, Danny
Esselman, Richèl Lubbers, Peterine
Arts

DOCK ROAD AREA
IJMUIDEN (NL)
2003 (study)
Urban plan; 650 houses and
apartments, shops, restaurants,
bars, workshops, parking garages,
dunes
15 hectare, 110,000 m²
Ton Venhoeven, Jos-Willem van
Oorschot, Arjen Zaal, Michael
Schwaiger

UNIVERSITY OF GRONINGEN (RUG)
GRONINGEN (NL)
2003 (study)
Faculty of Medical Science
6,750 m2
Ton Venhoeven, Jos-Willem van
Oorschot, Erwin Hilbrands

HOGEWEIJ
WEESP (NL)
2003 – 2005 (proposal)
Urban restructuring plan; apartments,
shopping centre, offices, restaurants,
elementary schools, nursery, day care
centre, parking garages
20 hectare
Ton Venhoeven, Bas Römgens, Arjen
Zaal, Cécilia Gross, Suzanne Andrée,
Peter Heideman

VENHOEVENCS.NL
2003 – 2005 (realized)
Website
Ton Venhoeven, Bas Römgens in
collaboration with graphic design
Studio LSD Simon Davies, Lauran
Schijvens

TOWN HALL
ZAANSTAD (NL)
2003 (study)
Bus station and town hall
20,000 m²
Ton Venhoeven, Arjen Zaal, Jos-
Willem van Oorschot, Aukje van
Bezeij, in collaboration with
Itten+Brechbuehl Architects AG (CH)

LABORATORY
UNIVERSITY OF GRONINGEN (RUG)
GRONINGEN (NL)
2003 (study)
Laboratory building
10,000 m²
Ton Venhoeven, Kees Plomp, Jos-
Willem van Oorschot

FIRE STATION
ENSCHEDE (NL)
2003 (study)
Fire station; garage, offices, fitness
room, storage room, workshops,
exercise room, living room, bedrooms
5,000 m²
Ton Venhoeven, Arjen Zaal

VAN HASSELTKANAAL
AMSTERDAM (NL)
2003 (study)
Bascule bridge; bridge for cars,
bicycles, pedestrians, 102 m.
Ton Venhoeven, Bas Römgens, Jos-
Willem van Oorschot

HOUSING
MUIDEN (NL)
2003 – 2005 (proposal)
Urban plan; apartments, houses,
villas, houses for elderly people,
community service centre, car park
3.4 hectare
Ton Venhoeven, Bas Römgens, Arjen
Zaal, Erwin Hilbrands, Suzanne
Andrée

ABRIXAS
AMSTERDAM (NL)
EINDHOVEN (NL)
2003 – 2004 (realized)
Video project; part of the opera
'Abrixas, passion of a satellite'
Ton Venhoeven, Bas Römgens, in
collaboration with artistic director
Titus Muizelaar, librettist Edzard Mik,
music composer Guus Janssen,
singer performer Jannie Pranger,
electronic performers Huib Emmer
and Edwin der Heide, Peter van
Bergen

LA SABBIA
UTRECHT (NL)
2004 – 2007 (proposal, to be
realized)
Bodyshape, dance and fitness centre;
fitness area, dance room, aerobics,
spinning, dojo, sauna, shop,
restaurant, apartments, parking
garage
5,666 m2
Ton Venhoeven, Peter Heideman, Kees
Plomp, Lydia Fraaije, Jos-Willem van
Oorschot, Tanja Djordjevic, Koen Smit

MINERVA DENTAL CLINIC
AMSTERDAM (NL)
2004 (proposal)
Dentist practice; treatment rooms,
reception area, service rooms,
waiting area
150 m²
Ton Venhoeven, Arjen Zaal, Cécilia
Gross

KALININGRAD
ZAANSTAD (NL)
2004 – present (proposal)
Office building; offices, car park
6,700 m²
Ton Venhoeven, Arjen Zaal, Jos-
Willem van Oorschot, Kees Plomp

LAUWERSOOG
DE MARNE (NL)
2004 (study)
Urban development plan for harbour;
leisure, tourism, industry and harbour
facilities, education centre, laboratory for sustainable development
100 hectare
Ton Venhoeven, Jos-Willem van
Oorschot, in collaboration with 'coast
wise' architect and urban planner Jan
de Graaf

EUROPEAN PATENT OFFICE
RIJSWIJK (NL)
2004 (proposal)
Office building; offices, auditoriums,
facilities, gardens
67,000 m²
Ton Venhoeven, Peter Heideman,
Kees Plomp, Jos-Willem van
Oorschot, Manfred Wansink, Cécilia
Gross, Peterine Arts, Willem
Lucassen, Suzanne Andree, in
collaboration with Itten+Brechbuehl
Architects AG

FOM AMOLF
AMSTERDAM (NL)
2004 (study)
Laboratory of physics; laboratories,
offices
8,000 m²
Ton Venhoeven, Manfred Wansink,
Jos-Willem van Oorschot

CORE HOSPITAL
ROTTERDAM (NL)
2004 (study)
open competition 'Future hospitals:
competitive and healing'
Innovative hospital concept; compact
general hospital, shops, theatre,
parking garage
21,000 m² + hotel, commercial
functions, parking garage
Ton Venhoeven, Peterine Arts, Cécilia
Gross, in collaboration with
Itten+Brechbuehl Architects AG (CH)
and BM Advise (NL)

BRIDGE
HOORN (NL)
2004 (study)
Bicycle bridge and café 250 m.
Ton Venhoeven, Erik de Vries, Jos-
Willem van Oorschot, Manfred
Wansink, Vani Vaitheeswaran

PROVOLTA
BASEL (CH)
2004 (study)
Urban development plan; apartments,
office space, clinic, shops,
restaurant, bar, supermarket, hotel,
library, sports centre, parking garage
4 hectare
Ton Venhoeven, Peterine Arts, Cécilia
Gross, Willem Lucassen

THE SILVER SWAN
UTRECHT (NL)
2004 – 2008 (realized)
Apartment building; 22 apartments,
parking garage
4,100 m²
Ton Venhoeven, Jos-Willem van
Oorschot, Manfred Wansink, Erwin
Hilbrands, Danny Esselman, Peter
Heideman, Arjen Zaal, Kees Plomp

KABOUTERCLUSTER
AMSTERDAM (NL)
2005 (study)
Elementary schools for handicapped
children
3,250 m²
Ton Venhoeven, Jos-Willem van
Oorschot

293

Swimming pool
Noordwijk (NL)

Imares
Den Helder (NL)

THE IN-BETWEEN TIME
THE HAGUE (NL)
2005 (study)
Urban development plan and proposal
for intermediate use of open areas at
Scheveningen Harbour; exhibition at
Stroom
27 hectare
Ton Venhoeven, Bas Römgens, in
collaboration with 'coastwise'
architect and urban planner Jan de
Graaf

PAUL STRADINS
UNIVERSITY HOSPITAL
RIGA (LV)
2005 (study)
University Hospital and campus; Core
Hospital with diagnostic spaces,
outpatient department, operating
theatres, intensive care units, trauma
centre, nurseries, clinics, hotel,
laboratories, research spaces,
auditoriums, restaurants, cafés,
seminar rooms, medical practices,
student housing, offices, parking
garage, city park
171,905 m²
Ton Venhoeven, Bas Römgens, in
collaboration with Itten+Brechbuehl
Architects AG

COMMUNITY SCHOOL IJBURG
AMSTERDAM (NL)
2005 (study)
Community school
Ton Venhoeven, Jos-Willem van
Oorschot, Peterine Arts

HIGHWAY A4
MIDDEN DELFLAND (NL)
2005 (proposal)
Highway design; highway, viaducts,
tunnel, bicycle bridges, sound
screens, landscape integration, 7 km.
Ton Venhoeven, Arjen Zaal, Bas
Römgens, Cecilia Gross in
collaboration with landscape
architects H+N+S

ATRIUM SANTÉ
HEERLEN (NL)
2005 (study)
Hospital; redevelopment Master plan
8,000 m² + 39,000 m² renovation
Ton Venhoeven, Peterine Arts, in
collaboration with Itten+Brechbuehl
Architects AG, and Maurer United
Architects

CITY OF CITIES
CHUNGCHEONGNAM (KR)
2005 (study)
Urban plan; energy producing,
autarkic city, 500,000 inhabitants,
200,000 workplaces, leisure
facilities, urban facilities, roads,
underground railway system, train
station, urban agriculture, landscape
18 km² + 55 km² nature development
Ton Venhoeven, Jos-Willem van
Oorschot, Manfred Wansink, in
collaboration with urban planners Ton
Schaap and Herman Zonderland DRO
Amsterdam, 3D designer Cees van
Giessen, urban planner René Kuiken,
professor Boudewijn Walraven,
University of Leiden

ZLTO
TILBURG (NL)
2005 (study)
Head office of agricultural
organization and parking garage
6,370 m²
Ton Venhoeven, Danny Esselman,
Cécilia Gross in collaboration with
marketing advisor Layana Mokoginta,
Purpura

ELECTRA
BASEL (CH)
2005 (proposal)
Multipurpose building; apartments,
supermarket, shops, offices,
restaurant, parking garage
22,610 m²
Ton Venhoeven, Peterine Arts, Jos-
Willem van Oorschot, Cécilia Gross,
Manfred Wansink, Kees Plomp

OFFICE BUILDING
ABU DHABI (VAE)
2005 (study)
Office building; offices and facilities
67,000 m²
Ton Venhoeven, Cécilia Gross, Jos-
Willem van Oorschot, in collaboration
with Itten+Brechbuehl Architects AG

INTERNATIONAL CRIMINAL COURT
THE HAGUE (NL)
2005 (architectural advise)
Ton Venhoeven, Richèl Lubbers

HIGHWAY A4
AMSTERDAM (NL) – ANTWERP (B)
2006 – 2007 (proposal, to be
realized)
Development plan; development plan
for highway, nodes, viaducts, flyovers,
ecoducts (viaducts for animals),
bicycle bridges, tunnels, sound
screens, city development guidelines,
landscape development, 140 km.
Ton Venhoeven, Arjen Zaal, Tim
Habraken, Bas Römgens, in
collaboration with landscape
architects H+N+S

THERESIA
TILBURG (NL)
2006 (study)
Multipurpose community school
5,000 m²
Ton Venhoeven, Jos-Willem van
Oorschot

ARNHEM SAKSEN WEIMAR
ARNHEM (NL)
2006 (proposal)
Urban plan; 450 apartments, houses,
studios
19 hectare
Ton Venhoeven, Jos-Willem van
Oorschot, Arjen Zaal, Peter Heideman
With urban planners and landscape
architects RBOI and project developer
VORM

COMMUNITY SCHOOL
LEIDEN (NL)
2006 – present (proposal, to be
realized)
Multipurpose community school and
apartments; 4 elementary schools,
library, neighbourhood centre, health
centre, nursery, gymnasium,
apartments, parking garage, bridges,
city square
23,000 m2
Ton Venhoeven, Arjen Zaal, Danny
Esselman, Kees Plomp, Cécilia
Gross, Wouter de Haas, Roland
Herpel, Tanja Djordjevic, Maarten
Bax, Urs Hasenberg, Niels Boswinkel,
Tim Habraken, Maidie van den Bos,
Pedro Torneiro

JAVA ISLAND SCHOOL
AMSTERDAM (NL)
2006 (study)
Community school
3,500 m²
Ton Venhoeven, Bas Römgens

SWIMMING POOL
NOORDWIJK (NL)
2006 (proposal)
Swimming pool, fitness, spa, health
clinic, parking garage
8,000 m²
Ton Venhoeven, Jos-Willem van
Oorschot, Cécilia Gross, Kees Plomp,
Danny Esselman

BRIDGE CARRASCOPLEIN
TELEPORT AMSTERDAM (NL)
2006 – present (proposal, to be
realized)
Bicycle and pedestrian bridge, 106 m.
Ton Venhoeven, Danny Esselman, Tim
Habraken, Roland Herpel

GGNET
APELDOORN (NL)
2006 – present (proposal, to be
realized)
Master plan for clinic and houses;
redevelopment of psychiatric care
centre with care clusters and
facilities, sports centre, farm,
greenhouse, apartments, houses and
parking
32 hectare
Ton Venhoeven, Bas Römgens, Lydia
Fraaije, Alondra Vargas, Anne
Moldenhauer

UMCG MASTERPLAN
GRONINGEN (NL)
2006 (study)
Master plan and psychiatric hospital
5 hectare + 9,000 m²
Ton Venhoeven, Bas Römgens, in
collaboration with Itten+Brechbuehl
Architects AG

KRUIDENBUURT
TILBURG (NL)
2006 – 2007 (study)
Multipurpose community school
5,000 m²
Ton Venhoeven, Tim Habraken

IMARES
DEN HELDER (NL)
2006 – present (proposal, to be
realized)
Laboratory building
4,200 m²
Ton Venhoeven, Jos-Willem van
Oorschot, Kees Plomp, Peter
Heideman, Lydia Fraaije, Martijn
Schlatmann, Jan Lebbink, Bas
Römgens

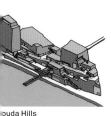

ouda Hills
ouda (NL)

usthof
oermond (NL)

nt Nicolaaslyceum
nsterdam (NL)

wimming pool Ypenburg
he Hague (NL)

agnerplein
lburg (NL)

LELYLAAN STATION
AMSTERDAM (NL)
2006 – present (proposal, to be realized)
Urban plan for station area and new office building; offices, station, bicycle shed, parking garage
11,000 m²
Ton Venhoeven, Bas Römgens, Peter Heideman, Tim Habraken, Thomas Stini, Manfred Wansink

DELFLANDPLEIN
AMSTERDAM (NL)
2006 (study)
Community school and apartments
11,000 m²
Ton Venhoeven, Arjen Zaal

GOUDA HILLS
GOUDA (NL)
2007 – present (proposal, to be realized)
Urban plan and leisure centre; apartments, restaurants, bars, leisure facilities, parking garage
35,000 m²
Ton Venhoeven, Jos-Willem van Oorschot, Roland Herpel

SWIMMING POOL YPENBURG
THE HAGUE (NL)
2007 – present (proposal, to be realized)
Swimming pool; olympic size indoor swimming pool, facilities
9,000 m²
Ton Venhoeven, Jos-Willem van Oorschot, Danny Esselman, Kees Plomp, Tim Habraken, Niels Boswinkel, Manfred Wansink, Lydia Fraaije, Roland Herpel, Bas Römgens, Martijn Schlatmann

TERWIJDE
UTRECHT (NL)
2007 – present (proposal, to be realized)
Urban plan and housing project; apartments, villa's, facilities, parking garage, garden
14,850 m²
Ton Venhoeven, Manfred Wansink, Kees Plomp, Ornella Lazzari, Tanja Djordjevic, Lydia Fraaije

OOSTERHEEM
ZOETERMEER (NL)
2007 (study)
Community school; 4 elementary schools, gymnasium, child day care centre, apartments
15,000 m²
Ton Venhoeven, Cécilia Gross, Kees Plomp, Jurriën van Duijkeren, Tim Habraken

LAAN VAN SPARTAAN
AMSTERDAM (NL)
2007 (study)
Pop music centre; auditorium, sports hall, bars, commercial spaces, apartments
15,460 m²
Ton Venhoeven, Cécilia Gross, Jos-Willem van Oorschot

KOP DIJKSGRACHT
CULTURAL CENTRE
AMSTERDAM (NL)
2007 (study)
Cultural centre, restaurants, urban agriculture, theatre
5,050 m²
Ton Venhoeven, Jos Willem van Oorschot

OPERATING CENTRE
MAASBRACHT (NL)
2007 (proposal, supervision)
Urban plan for an operating centre for bridges and locks
2,040 m²
Ton Venhoeven, Tim Habraken

GGNET WARNSVELD
ZUTPHEN (NL)
2007 – present (proposal, to be realized)
Master plan; psychiatric care centre, care facilities, service apartments
16 hectare
Ton Venhoeven, Bas Römgens, Lydia Fraaije

WAGNERPLEIN
TILBURG (NL)
2007 – present (proposal, to be realized)
Multipurpose sports centre; swimming pools, fitness, sports hall, bar, restaurant, extracurricular child day care centre
11,600 m²
Ton Venhoeven, Manfred Wansink, Jos-Willem van Oorschot, Bas Römgens, Kees Plomp, Danny Esselman, Cécilia Gross, Lydia Fraaije, Thomas Stini, Roland Herpel, Tanja Djordjevic

LEISURE CENTRE
VIANEN (NL)
2007 (study)
Multipurpose leisure centre; indoor swimming pools, fitness, sports hall, bowling centre, dojo, dance school, child day care centre, youth centre, social cultural facilities, theatre, bar, restaurant, parking garage
19,000 m²
Ton Venhoeven, Tim Habraken, Kees Plomp, Jurriën van Duijkeren

LUSTHOF
ROERMOND (NL)
2007 (study)
Master plan; conversion of former courthouse and prison to apartments, offices, shops, spa, bars, restaurant, courtyards, gardens
10,435 m²
Ton Venhoeven, Lydia Fraaije, Jos-Willem van Oorschot, Manfred Wansink, in collaboration with project developer Erfgoedwonen, and restoration architect Verlaan & Bouwstra, Peter Mattie, Insight and historic advise Bureau M&DM

STEINERBOS
STEIN (NL)
2007 (study)
Sustainable entertainment park and swimming pool; indoor swimming pool, health centre, park, leisure facilities
6,050 m2 + 25 hectare
Ton Venhoeven, Bas Römgens, Manfred Wansink, Lydia Fraaije, in collaboration with B+B landscape architects

VELSERTUNNEL
VELZEN-NOORD (NL)
2007 (study)
Urban plan for an operating centre of bridges and locks, 1,500 m.
Ton Venhoeven, Tim Habraken, Alondra Vargas

PAUL STRADINS
UNIVERSITY HOSPITAL
RIGA (LV)
2007 – present
Master plan development; architectural and organizational advise
Ton Venhoeven, Bas Römgens, in collaboration with Itten + Brechbuehl AG architects, and JKMM architects

SINT NICOLAASLYCEUM
AMSTERDAM (NL)
2007 (study)
High School; school, atrium, sports hall, restaurant, theatre, media centre, roof garden, sports courts
12,900 m²
Ton Venhoeven, Manfred Wansink, Jos-Willem van Oorschot, in collaboration with Itten + Brechbuehl AG architects

KATWIJK LEISURE CENTRE
KATWIJK (NL)
2007 – present (proposal, to be realized)
Leisure building; swimming pools, sports hall, fitness club, table tennis facilities, restaurant
11,000 m²
Ton Venhoeven, Kees Plomp, Tim Habraken, Dion Lembekker

SHOPPING CENTRE
HOLENDRECHT (NL)
2007 (study)
Shopping centre, apartments, offices
9,000 m²
Ton Venhoeven, Tim Habraken, Alondra Vargas

HOSPITAL
ALKMAAR (NL)
2007 (study)
Urban plan for redevelopment of hospital and neighbourhood
100,000 m²
Ton Venhoeven, Tanja Djordjevic, Lydia Fraaije, Bas Römgens

PIED À TERRE VAN DER GRIFT
AMSTERDAM (NL)
2007 – present (proposal, to be realized)
Pied à terre, home cinema, office, bed & breakfast apartment
33 m²
Ton Venhoeven, Cécilia Gross, Kim van den Hoven, Ornella Lazzari, Tim Habraken

ST. JOEP
ROERMOND (NL)
2007 (study)
Urban plan for houses, apartments, parking garage, courtyards
10,000 m²
Ton Venhoeven, Lydia Fraaije

CITROËN GARAGES
AMSTERDAM (NL)
2007 (study)
Conversion and extension; cultural centre and creative industry
12,000 m²
Ton Venhoeven, Jos-Willem van Oorschot, Thomas Stini

**CRUQUIUSHOEVE
CRUQUIUS (NL)**
2007 – present (proposal, to be realized)
Urban Master plan; houses, apartments, villa's, epileptic care centre, epileptic hospital, landscape, infrastructure
52 hectare
Ton Venhoeven, Bas Römgens, Ornella Lazzari

**ZICHTFLATS
HOEK VAN HOLLAND (NL)**
2008 – present (proposal, to be realized)
Urban Master plan; redevelopment houses, apartments,
Ton Venhoeven, Bas Römgens, Thomas Stini

**ZOP
HAARLEMMERMEER (NL)**
2008 (study)
Medical facilities, offices
Ton Venhoeven, Bas Römgens, Thomas Stini

**HOUSE
BLARICUM (NL)**
2008 – present (study)
Private house
500 m2
Ton Venhoeven, Lydia Fraaije

**CHINESE HOTEL
AMSTERDAM (NL)**
2008 – present (study)
Ton Venhoeven, Lydia Fraaije

**CUBIC HOUSE
TERWIJDE (NL)**
2008 (study)
Ton Venhoeven, Tim Habraken, Lydia Fraaije, Martijn Schlatmann, Anna Lea Kaufhold

**STATIONSKNOOP NOORD
AMSTERDAM (NL)**
2008 – present (study)
Ton Venhoeven, Bas Römgens, Martijn Schlatmann, Martijn van Sluijters

**MUIDERPOORTSTATION
AMSTERDAM (NL)**
2008 – present (proposal, to be realized)
Urban plan
Ton Venhoeven, Katharina Hagg, Lydia Fraaije, Ornella Lazzari, Sylvain Wintz, Bas Römgens

**THERMEN
ALPHEN AAN DEN RIJN (NL)**
2008 – 2009 (study)
Swimming pool
Ton Venhoeven, Bas Römgens, Manfred Wansink, Martijn van Sluijters, Jan Lebbink, Ornella Lazzari

**SWIMMING POOL
DEN HELDER (NL)**
2008 – present (study)
Ton Venhoeven, Kees Plomp, Maarten Bax, Jan Lebbink

**RECREATION PARK DE WARANDE
WETTEREN (B)**
2008 – present (proposal)
Urban plan, sports hall
Ton Venhoeven, Katharina Hagg, Ornella Lazzari, Sylvain Wintz, Maarten Bax, Bas Römgens in cooperation with Archi+I architekten and Marie-Laure Hoedemakers landscape architects

**SPORTFORUM
ROOSENDAAL (NL)**
2009 – present (proposal, to be realized)
Sports centre; sports hall, gym, dance hall, fitness, gym, restaurant, facilities
5,000 m²
Ton Venhoeven, Manfred Wansink, Maarten Bax

**COMMUNITY SCHOOL OUDELAND
ROTTERDAM (NL)**
2009 – present (proposal, to be realized)
Community school; 2 schools, day care centre, sports facilities, after school centre, community centre
4,719 m²
Ton Venhoeven, Cécilia Gross, Jan Lebbink, Bas Römgens

**MFA BISONSPOOR
MAARSEN (NL)**
2009 (study)
Multifunctional leisure centre; swimming pool, sports facilities, library, youth centre, 40 dwellings, restaurant
6,955 m²
Ton Venhoeven, Cécilia Gross, Danny Esselman, Jan Lebbink

We are very grateful for all employees who contributed to our works over the years. In case we failed to mention someone who worked on a specific project, please contact the office so we can make corrections in future prints or editions of this publication.

Cubic House
Terwijde (NL)

Stationsknoop Noord
Amsterdam (NL)

Thermen
Alphen aan den Rijn (NL)